Regulation of the market in the National Health Service

Competition and the common good

Edited by
Anthony Hopkins
Director, Research Unit, Royal College of Physicians

1994

300921 2T

ROYAL COLLEGE OF PHYSICIANS OF LONDON

Acknowledgements

This book results from a workshop organised by the Research Unit of the Royal College of Physicians on behalf of the Conference of Medical Royal Colleges and their Faculties in the United Kingdom and the National Health Service Management Executive. The programme was arranged by Alan Langlands and Anthony Hopkins. The editor is grateful to those colleagues who contributed background papers, and to all participants who contributed to the discussion. All contributions have been edited.

The Research Unit of the Royal College of Physicians is supported by generous grants from the Wolfson and Welton Foundations, by other charitable donations, and by the Department of Health.

940331

Royal College of Physicians of London
11 St Andrews Place, London NW1 4LE

Registered Charity No. 210508

Copyright © 1994 Royal College of Physicians of London
ISBN 1 873240 64 3

Typeset by Dan-Set Graphics, Telford, Shropshire
Printed in Great Britain by Cathedral Print Services Ltd, Salisbury

Members of the Workshop

Indicates authors of papers prepared for the workshop and published in the volume.

Martin Buxton *Professor of Health Economics, Health Economics Research Group, Department of Economics, University of West London, Uxbridge, Middlesex UB8 3PH.*

Bruce Campbell *Consultant Surgeon, Royal Devon and Exeter Hospital, Barrack Road, Wonford, Exeter EX2 5DW.*

*__Ian Carruthers__ *Chief Executive, Dorset Health Commission, Victoria House, Princes Road, Ferndown, Dorset BH22 9JR.*

Malcolm Clarke *Chief Executive, Salford Family Health Services Authority, The Willows, Lord's Avenue, Salford M5 2JR.*

Peter Coe *District General Manager, East London and the City Health Authority, Tredegar House, 97-99 Bow Road, London E3 2AN.*

Brendan Devlin *Chairman, Surgical Audit and Quality Assurance Committee, Surgical Audit Unit, Royal College of Surgeons of England, 35-43 Lincoln's Inn Fields, London WC2A 3PN.*

Stuart Dickens *Chief Executive, South Birmingham District Health Authority, District Headquarters, 27 Highfield Road, Edgbaston, Birmingham B15 3DP.*

Sir William Doughty *Chairman, North West Thames Regional Health Authority, 40 Eastbourne Terrace, London W2 3QR.*

Len Fenwick *Chief Executive, Freeman Group of Hospitals National Health Service Trust, High Heaton, Newcastle upon Tyne NE7 7DN.*

*__John Grimley Evans__ *Professor of Geriatric Medicine, Nuffield Department of Clinical Medicine, Geriatric Medicine Division, Radcliffe Infirmary, Oxford OX2 6HE.*

Peter Shrigley *Chief Executive, Royal Oldham Hospital and Community Services National Health Service Trust, Westhulme Avenue, Oldham, Lancashire OL1 2PN.*

*Clive Smee *Chief Economic Adviser, Department of Health, Room 2811, Millbank Tower, 21-24 Millbank, London SW1P 4QU.*

John Sully *Chief Executive, Eastbourne Health Authority, 9 Upperton Road, Eastbourne, East Sussex BN21 2BH.*

David Taylor *Senior Manager, Health Studies, Audit Commission, 1 Vincent Square, London SW1P 2PN.*

Richard Thomson *Senior Lecturer in Public Health Medicine, School of Health Care Sciences, The Medical School, 11 Framlington Place, Newcastle upon Tyne NE2 4HH.*

David Tod *President, National Association of Fundholding General Practitioners, 12 Durham Road, Raynes Park, London SW20 0TW.*

Alan Torbet *General Manager, Birmingham Family Health Service Authority, Aston Cross, 50 Rocky Lane, Aston, Birmingham B6 5RQ.*

*Tom Treasure *Cardiac and Thoracic Surgeon, St George's Hospital, Blackshaw Road, London SW17 0QT.*

Graham Winyard *Medical Director, National Health Service Management Executive, Quarry House, Quarry Hill, Leeds LS2 7UE.*

Tera Younger *Purchasing Development Manager, South West Thames Regional Health Authority, 40 Eastbourne Terrace, London W2 3QR.*

Contents

Introduction

The NHS and Community Care Act 1990, foreshadowed by the White Paper *Working for Patients* a year earlier, separated the purchase or commission of health services from their provision. Until then, regional health authorities (now to be phased out) and through them health districts and district general hospitals had been allocated budgets on the basis of need, estimated through formulas first introduced by the Resource Allocation Working Party in 1976, and subsequently modified to take better account of morbidity. Unfortunately, the harder that clinicians in a hospital worked, the more they drove their hospital into overspending their budgets, a problem that became more and more acute in the early 1980s. At about the same time, there was a general perception that health services were relatively unresponsive to the wishes of their users, that innovations such as day case surgery were slow to be introduced long after their cost-effectiveness had been proven, and that there were embedded inefficiencies in the service. The introduction of general management as a result of the Griffiths Enquiry in 1983 certainly sharpened the focus of more effective management, but the strains continued, until the 1990 Act instituted an entirely new way of financial allocation through purchasers to competitive providers of services which compete for contracts to deliver care. By the end of 1994, it is estimated that more than 90% of NHS services (other than general practitioners who may be both fundholders and providers of services) will be managed by some 440 hospital or community trusts.

In a truly national National Health Service, some sort of regulation is necessary to ensure that provision through these independent trusts together fulfil all needs for health care. It has never been thought that competition alone would be capable of this. The purpose of the workshop on which this book is based was, therefore, to explore what 'higher level' regulation is necessary in order to manage the total market place in order to ensure that the appropriate health care needs of the population are met and that adequate programmes for health promotion and for the prevention of disease are in place.

The workshop and the editing of this book took place against

the background of the review, set up by the Secretary of State for
Health, of the structure, functions and manpower required to
ensure that the government's reforms of the NHS are fully implemented; to ensure effective oversight of both purchasers and
providers; to ensure that the Secretary of State is able to discharge
her statutory responsibilities for the NHS; and to ensure that the
proportion of NHS expenditure devoted to direct patient care is
maximised. The review, published in October 1993, will result in
the abolition of the 14 statutory regional health authorities, and in
the reorganisation of the NHS Management Executive to include
eight regional offices, each headed by a regional director, to
replace both the old regional health authorities and the existing
outposts of the Management Executive, together known as the
intermediate tier. Other main features of the review include the
development of stronger purchasing by enabling district health
authorities and family health service authorities to merge (thereby
integrating purchasing across primary and secondary care boundaries), and the appointment of eight regional non-executive members to the NHS Policy Board. The Secretary of State has also
determined that the central management of the NHS should
remain within the Department of Health. The NHS Management
Executive, operating within the Department will develop a clearer
identity as the 'headquarters' of the NHS.

The Secretary of State's review recognises the need to develop
and regulate the market, and to 'manage' purchasers and
providers. In para. 35, the review states that 'NHS central management will have the responsibility for setting the rules which
determine the structure of the NHS internal market, and for establishing a 'minimum set' of regulations covering financial arrangements, pricing and quality. The regional offices will play the key
role in ensuring compliance with the regulatory framework in
their regions, and, where necessary, arbitrating in case of contract
disputes between purchasers and providers'. In para 36 the review
states '. . . NHS central management must ensure that each health
authority is purchasing efficiently and effectively', and in para 39,
'. . . Clear criteria will be developed to define the circumstances in
which it is appropriate for central management to intervene to
ensure that providers fulfil wider national policy objectives.'

The review therefore acknowledges the need both for regulation
of the market, and for the management of purchasers and
providers, themes further developed in the contributions and discussions that follow. Surprisingly little editorial annotation has
been necessary to ensure that the papers and discussion are

relevant to the revised management structure, perhaps because participants largely foresaw the likely merger of regional health authorities and Management Executive outposts, and of district and family health service authorities.

The workshop was sponsored jointly by the NHS Management Executive and the Conference of Medical Royal Colleges and their Faculties in the United Kingdom. It was arranged on their joint behalf by the Research Unit of the Royal College of Physicians, which has a long standing interest in the effective and efficient delivery of health services, and in the measurement of the quality of medical care. It is good that clinicians and health service managers are jointly concerned in discussions such as these.

Background papers on a number of key areas were circulated to workshop participants before the meeting. The discussion on the papers was tape-recorded, but both have been edited in order to provide a more coherent form and readable text.

ANTHONY HOPKINS
Research Unit
Royal College of Physicians
London

ALAN LANGLANDS
Chief Executive Designate
NHS Management Executive
Leeds

1 | The background to the National Health Service reforms of 1989/1990

Ian Carruthers

Chief Executive, Dorset Health Commission

The White Paper *Working for Patients* published in 1989 introduced the notion of competition as a means of improving the efficiency, effectiveness and distribution of health care. For some years it had become evident that changes were necessary in the National Health Service (NHS). Major variations in performance had developed between hospitals, primary care and community health service organisations providing care. Providers were also considered to be slow to respond to the needs of users in terms of quality and service delivery. There was also a need for better use of nationally limited resources and better organisational performance. This was typified by a hospital with capacity to treat more patients but without funding to do so. Because activity and income were not linked, the treatment of increased numbers of patients sometimes resulted in expenditure exceeding the centrally allocated budget, leading to further reduction in services to achieve financial control. Health professionals became demotivated through such apparent stop/go policies.

The NHS reforms introduced by the National Health Service and Community Care Act 1990 have brought new underlying values, which should drive purchasers of health care. These include:

1. The separation of funding of health services from their provision, so that health authorities focus on identifying the needs of their populations and on meeting them through contracts with providers of care. This has led to a more critical assessment of the services required, and introduced a driving force for change.
2. The creation of general practitioner fundholding and NHS trusts, which are new mechanisms to facilitate local changes.
3. Changes in the funding system so that money follows patients, and hospitals and community health services are funded on the basis of the activity undertaken. Better performance is thereby rewarded, and there are incentives to improve the quality of service and to utilise spare capacity.

1

4. The development of joint agencies to commission care. These should achieve improved health and the delivery of health services by pooling resources for the more effective integrated purchasing of primary and secondary care.
5. The promotion of more choice for individuals who are waiting for treatment, to enable them to gain faster access to care.
6. Increased accountability of individuals and organisations by the establishment of management through contract rather than by hierarchy.

The creation of an internal market in which purchasers and providers come together and contract for services of high quality that give value for money was seen as an opportunity to introduce competition; this was thought likely to benefit patient care and improve the delivery of health services. However, the market must evolve and develop. Incentives for improving efficiency and service responsiveness include:

• ending the conflict of interest in combining purchasing and service provision in one organisation;
• enabling purchasers to improve their performance by concentrating on being responsive and efficient agents for individual patients and populations;
• enabling providers to become more effective and efficient through competition and through a contracting relationship which defines standards of quality and output; and
• encouraging better performance by providers so that continual improvement in care is achieved without the necessity to switch services between good and poor performers.

The purpose of this workshop was to consider a framework in which the maximum benefits of competition can be gained, and to consider the necessary limitations of competition by regulation to ensure that the gains accrue to the health of the nation as a whole.

2 | The market in health care

Clive Smee
Chief Economic Adviser, Department of Health, London

The White Paper *Working for Patients*[1] aimed to introduce the incentives of market relationships and market behaviour into hospital and secondary health care—a publicly owned sector of the economy that had previously relied on command relationships. Greater competition had been introduced into primary care through the earlier White Paper, *Promoting better Health,*[2] which did not propose a separate purchasing function, perhaps in part because patients were thought capable of choosing between largely autonomous general practitioners and dentists, without the aid of purchasing agents acting on their behalf. This chapter concentrates on the market for hospital services.

Some of the structural features of the market in secondary care are now in place:

- separation of purchasers and providers;
- some autonomy for providers;
- contractual relationships instead of hierarchies;
- new pricing and cost systems.

Structural changes are still occurring, particularly on the purchasing side, such as mergers of district health authorities, joint commissioning and more general practitioners becoming fundholders. These changes may be diverting energies away from identifying new suppliers or new markets. Moreover, to ensure a smooth transition, many of the controls and disciplines of the old command systems have been maintained. The operation of market forces has so far generally been confined to areas in which they do not threaten the financial viability of existing institutions. Competitive markets largely work through putting the financial viability of existing providers under continual threat, so it is clear that market forces are currently severely constrained.

What kind of market?

Rather than describe the current nature of the secondary care

3

'market', it may be more helpful to consider the kind of market there is likely to be when the structural changes slow down, the behavioural adjustments work through, *and* assuming there will be a shift from central controls and disciplines to greater reliance on market forces. The purpose of introducing market mechanisms into the health service was to improve efficiency and responsiveness, so one approach to this question is to examine how far the secondary health care system in the UK already has, or can easily develop, the features that characterise efficient markets. These features fall under five headings:

- structure;
- ease of entry;
- information;
- motivation/incentives;
- risk selection.

Structure

It is generally argued that markets have to be competitive for services to be delivered in a way that is efficient, responsive and offers genuine choice. A competitive market is characterised as one with many providers, each unable to influence the market price by changing its output, and with many purchasers each unable to influence price by changing its purchases. How far can the internal market for health services reflect these characteristics? On the provider side, the extent of competition depends both on how the service is defined and on the size of the relevant market. Many district general hospitals outside conurbations appear to enjoy a monopoly position. But hospitals are multiproduct 'factories' or 'workshops'. The markets they serve can vary from the very small, for example, providing accident services within 14 minutes' travel time by ambulance, to the very large, for example, the whole country for some of the more rarely performed chemical pathology tests. The extent of competition is also sensitive to the scope for substitution. For example, unconventional suppliers may enter the market, such as fundholding general practitioners offering new clinics, or new organisational forms may be introduced, such as private accident centres.

This diversity may be captured by developing typologies that cover a range of different market structures. For example:

- monopolistic: ambulance services and many accident and emergency services may enjoy a high degree of monopoly power;

- oligopolistic (few sellers): other conventional acute services and regional specialties may be provided under oligopoly conditions;
- competitive: much elective surgery, some community services and pathology may face highly competitive markets.

There are signs of services moving between these categories. Competition is increasing, particularly for regional specialties and community/outreach services, but there remain uncertainties about the proportions of health services that fall, or are likely to fall, under each of these broad market headings.

An early study of the hospital market structure in the West Midlands suggested that by conventional criteria there is scope for a high degree of competition.[3] The Tomlinson inquiry attempted to assess the scale and range of inner London services at risk through outer London and shire purchasers switching their contracts elsewhere.[4] On the rough and ready assumptions used, a relatively small proportion of services was judged to be at risk. Even so, the potential impact on hospital cost structures and viability was considered severe. The Department of Health is currently using the 'Autoroute' mapping facility to identify travel to hospital markets, and the extent to which they overlap on different assumptions about acceptable travel times. More empirical work is needed but, given the large proportion of the population living in or near conurbations, it seems likely that few hospitals enjoy natural monopolies, though many—perhaps most—secondary care services are provided in markets that would be judged highly concentrated in structure by conventional criteria.

On the purchaser side of the market there is a contrast between the increasingly large health authorities, with a good deal of monopsony power, and the growing number of fundholding general practitioners, potentially in competition both with each other and with the health authorities. In terms of market efficiency, particularly from the perspective of users, it is generally thought that monopsony power (single purchaser) is less threatening than monopoly power (single provider). In theory, monopsonists who force prices too low will discourage innovation and new market entrants. Against this, large purchasers have advantages in terms of effective assessment of health need, proper planning and bulk purchasing, reflected in the current usage of the term 'commissioning' health care. There are also early signs that large purchasing consortia may be more successful in stimulating provider competition. However, the main problem with monopsony purchasers is that they have few incentives to be responsive to the needs and wants of the final users. This may be particularly true if there are not other forms of local accountability.

Large fundholding general practices in rural areas will also not be subject to effective market disciplines. In general though, fundholding general practitioners should face greater incentives than health authorities to be responsive and efficient, because patients can choose their practice (albeit within practical geographical limits). So far, the differences in reported behaviour of the two purchaser models seem to mirror the differences in their incentive structures.

Ease of entry

More recent economic thinking has tended to downplay the importance of large numbers of purchasers and providers as a precondition for efficient markets, and to emphasise instead the importance of ease of market entry. Even single suppliers may be forced to act efficiently if they think that attempts to extort excess profits will lead to new market entrants. If markets are to be contestable in this sense, the costs of entry must not be too high. In turn, this implies that capital costs must not be excessive and, in particular, that most of these costs can be readily recovered and that incumbents take time to respond to new challenges. The extent to which this is true will vary from service to service. In a small geographical area like the UK it may be possible in many cases for an existing provider to enter a new market by better use of, or a small expansion to, existing facilities.

Information

If health service providers are to compete in terms of price and quality rather than, say, marketing skills, then differences in price and quality must be perceptible to purchasers. In addition, if purchasers are to be encouraged to shop around, and the entry of new suppliers is to be facilitated, information on prices and quality should be readily available. Market pressures may in time generate pricing in terms of standard product units, such as Diagnosis Related Groups, and price lists may then be readily available. If not, there are good efficiency arguments for government intervention in favour of openness.

Information on costs and prices is improving but remains inadequate, leading many purchasers to rely on block contracts. This limits the extent to which money truly follows the patient, it saps provider (and particularly clinician) motivation, and also hinders the development of the more sophisticated product definitions and risk management behaviour that is required in a well-functioning market. Poor information on costs can also lead to an exaggeration—by purchasers if not by providers—of the extent to which costs are fixed, thus discouraging some purchasers from seeking more competitive suppliers, and enabling providers to avoid adjusting their cost structures.

However, the central information problem in health care markets, and indeed one of the major causes of 'failure' in such markets, is the absence of information on quality of service. It used to be argued that it was the imbalance in information about health outcomes between purchasers and providers that gave providers such monopoly power. It is now more widely appreciated that providers are also frequently unclear about both the clinical outcomes of the services they offer and the determinants of those outcomes. In these circumstances, with little or no reporting of actual outcomes, it is unsurprising that district purchasers (commissioners) show a tendency to treat waiting times and travel distances as the key elements in quality. For similar reasons, American patients and their agents have treated the sophistication of medical technology and the luxury of hospital hotel services as proxies for the quality of clinical care. To tackle this problem, Enthoven, and other supporters of managed competition in the USA, argue strongly for the creation of a national 'Outcomes Management Standards Board' that would set standards for outcomes reporting.[5]

In the UK, the lack of information on outcomes, effectiveness and cost effectiveness is being countered by a number of central initiatives. These include the Cochrane Centre for reviewing the results of randomised trials, the Outcomes Clearing House, the Bulletins for Effective Health Care and the epidemiologically based Needs Assessment Reports. How far these redress the imbalance of information will depend on the skills and knowledge of purchasers as well as on their bargaining power but, until there is widespread public reporting of outcomes, fundholding general practitioners will have major advantages over health authorities as purchasers. General practitioners see their patients before and after they receive hospital treatment, and therefore have direct information (admittedly on a small scale) on the quality of care of different providers. District health authorities can hope to build up such information (albeit potentially on a much larger scale) only as and when contracts require the reporting of clinical outcomes. In recognition of this argument, the Management Executive of the

NHS in Scotland is requiring a range of outcome measures—
including peri-operative death rates—to be included in hospital
contracts from 1993–94. The publication by *The Times* of crude
peri-operative death rates from hospitals in England led to a vigorous correspondence,[5] and to a leader in the *Lancet*[6] pointing out
that many technical factors have to be considered before such measures are helpful.[8]

Motivation

For a market to promote efficiency, providers must be motivated at
least in part by financial considerations. Under the current rules,
NHS trusts cannot survive unless they pay some attention to recov-
ering their costs. However, the cap on the rate of return they may
earn, taking one year with another, ensures that financial incentives are not as sharp as in for-profit organisations. These pricing
rules were established to prevent the exploitation of monopoly
power. It is too early to judge whether they are effective in doing so
and, at the same time, avoid unduly restricting innovation.

Further potential dampeners on the motivation of providers are
the limits on borrowing and the rules governing access to capital.
Capital charging has reduced the demand for capital, but the borrowing limits (or the criteria for allocating capital) are seen as preventing profitable developments. Incentives to innovate are bound
to be affected.

The difference between providers of health services and
providers in most normal markets is not the interest of their managers in financial issues but the difficulty that health service managers have in influencing the decisions of those who make the critical decisions about allocating resources: that is, the clinicians.
Despite the effort that has been put into organisational arrangements aimed at aligning clinician and manager interests, such as
the resource management initiative, and the development of clinical directorates,[7] major doubts remain as to how far the two groups
share a common understanding of, and commitment to, the kinds
of behaviour necessary for successful performance in an internal
market. The many reports of early exhaustion of provider budgets
for elective care may be due simply to poor financial reporting systems, but they could also reflect a failure to develop resource allocation systems under which clinicians feel they 'own' the surpluses
or losses they incur.

If markets are to improve efficiency and responsiveness, there
are also major implications for the motivation of purchasers who

must in particular be concerned to meet the needs of the final users of health care services, the patients. This raises two problems: first, there must be agreement on who defines the needs of patients. At present, several parties are accepted as having a role in defining needs:

- the Department of Health and the NHS Management Executive in laying down national targets;
- regions in setting any regional priorities;
- district purchasers through their needs assessment work;
- fundholding and other general practitioners;
- the patients themselves.

What is not clear is how these different views of patients' needs are to be balanced and whose views are expected to dominate in each set of circumstances. For example, when it comes to the allocation of resources, there is a trade-off between pursuing the targets of *The Health of the Nation*[8] and those of *The Patient's Charter*.[9] How is this trade-off to be made?

The second linked issue concerns who is best placed to identify patient needs and to use the information provided by patients. To the extent that priority is given to patients' needs as they define them themselves, general practitioner-based purchasing arrangements are likely to produce more responsive markets than arrangements based on larger and more distant agencies. However, if patient needs are defined in terms of the health needs of local populations, and public health specialists are the arbiters of those needs, purchasing authorities with district-wide responsibilities are likely to be judged better able to contribute to efficient and responsive markets.

The relations between principal and agent are a pervasive problem in modern societies. In the internal health market, there is a particular complication in that the purchasing agent is expected to be responsive to several different principals: the Department of Health, the NHS Management Executive, the regional health authority, the patient and (when not a fundholder) the general practitioner.

Risk selection

American experience suggests that one of the greatest threats to the ability of health care markets to deliver outcomes that are efficient for the health of the general population is risk selection—that is, the opportunity for purchasers and providers to succeed by selecting good risks and avoiding bad ones, rather than through improving quality and patient satisfaction. There are great differences in the costs of patients, both over a year and in the course of a single hospital episode, and thus major incentives to purchasers and providers to find ways to avoid taking responsibility for treating the more expensive patients. For example, American studies have suggested that the one per cent of patients with the highest costs in a given year can account for more than a quarter of total health service costs.[10]

On the purchasing side of the internal health market, the need for health authorities to take responsibility for *all* patients in a geographical area leaves them with few obvious opportunities to engage in any risk selection. However, they may become the victims of risk selection by fundholding general practitioners. Although there is not yet firm evidence of such behaviour, there are large financial incentives for fundholders to engage in 'cream-skimming'—that is, discrimination in favour of patients who will cost less over a period of time. Of course, if fundholders have as much difficulty in identifying the high risks as those responsible for the formula used in allocating budgets, there is no problem. The concern, which American experience suggests is well founded, is that fundholders will be better able than the funders to identify low and high risks. It is significant that two of the most knowledgeable and sympathetic analysts of general practitioner fundholding regard cream-skimming as a possible Achilles' heel of the whole scheme (H. Glennerster and M. Matsanganis: personal communications).

On the provider side of the market, the incentive to select patients according to their likely costs will again depend on the nature of the payment system. For example, where payment is on a single cost-per-treatment basis, consultants could be put under pressure to refer complicated cases elsewhere or, if they are already admitted, to discharge such patients prematurely. The professional nature of medical practice may of course be more than sufficient to offset these pressures.

Who are the key players in shaping market behaviour?

There are five broad categories of players in the internal market:

- patients;
- purchasers;
- providers;
- regulators;
- central policy makers.

A central idea in the NHS reforms was to tip the balance of power between providers and patients more in favour of patients. There were a number of reasons for separating off and institutionalising the purchasing function rather than passing it to the final users, as has happened in the new schools 'market', among which was the belief that people needing health care lack the knowledge and information to look after their own interests. Much of the pressure for regulation and for a separate regulatory function appears to stem from the view that purchasing agencies also cannot be relied upon fully to look after the interests of patients.

Patients

Patients are too easily forgotten when considering the workings of internal markets, perhaps because patient freedoms can be a restriction on clinical and management freedoms. However, their knowledge, energy and preferences can have a major impact on market behaviour. For example, well informed or opinionated patients can have a significant impact on the behaviour of purchasers (whether commissioning health authorities or fundholders). How patients trade off high-cost local services against lower-cost more distant services, or immediate access to more distant facilities against waiting for local services, or how far they can distinguish care of real quality from care that is simply expensive, will all affect either the scale of the market or the form that competition takes. Logically, if the intention of introducing an internal market is to make health care services more responsive to patients, priority should be given both to finding out what patients value and to giving them (and their friends and relatives) the information that will enable them to make clear their preferences.

Purchasing agents

For the foreseeable future, the sophistication of medical knowledge and the absence of clear signals of quality and outcome make it certain that patients will require purchasing agents to assist them in selecting appropriate services. The two types of purchasing agent introduced by the reforms—health authorities and fundholding general practitioners—are expected to be well informed about the needs of those whom they represent, and active in pursuing their best interests. The two models have markedly different strengths and weaknesses; how they evolve—whether as competitors, complements or co-ordinated purchasers—will have a major impact on market behaviour.

Cutting across the organisational differences, several underlying types of purchaser behaviour may be identified and labelled, somewhat mischievously, as:

- *protectionists* (or 'cosy relationists'): these appear to be primarily concerned to maintain the *status quo* so far as local providers are concerned;
- *autarkists:* these appear to be primarily concerned to establish local self-sufficiency in as wide a range of services as possible, usually on the grounds that this will minimise patient travelling time;
- *monopsonists:* these tend to concentrate on driving prices as low as possible, disregarding the effect on innovation and potential market entrants;
- *furniture movers:* these spend so much time changing the organisational structure of purchasing, or talking about it, that they do not get round to any active purchasing;
- *catalysts* (sometimes called *destabilisers*): a term commonly used to refer to fundholding general practitioners who have used their freedoms to shake up the local mould of provision;
- *relational activists:* those who are trying to build up longer-term relations, but only after carefully surveying the alternatives, and identifying providers, including new entrants to the market, who can meet their demanding standards.

How market behaviour develops will clearly depend on which of these categories of purchaser become most common. There will be different views on how purchasers currently divide in terms of these categories, but a guess would be that at present many fall under the headings of 'protectionists', 'autarkists' and 'furniture movers'. An efficient market requires that many more develop roles as 'catalysts' and 'relational activists' and are willing to encourage new entrants to create contestability. Most importantly, all purchasers, whatever their behavioural characteristics, need more information and better analytical tools if they are to act as effective counterweights to hospitals and other providers.

Providers

The third category of players, the providers, includes trusts, directly managed units, general practitioners, both fundholding and not, and the private sector. In most parts of the health service market, the skills and knowledge of this group currently give them a dominant position. How far and how fast this will change will depend both on the skills and behaviour of purchasers and on the extent to which the providers see their business as contestable, in the sense of being continually under the threat, if not the fact, of competition from other suppliers. The benefits that contestability would bring depend not only on the extent of 'slack' in current providers but also on how much freedom they have to respond to competitive threats. New Zealand managers who have worked both in public hospitals in New Zealand and in trusts in the UK believe that trust managers remain more constrained in the UK in the deployment of their resources, particularly in the efficient use of labour.

The regulators

The role of the fourth set of players, the regulators, is perhaps the least well defined, but it is a role for which several pretenders, the NHS Management Executive, regional offices of the Management Executive, purchasers and the professions, all claim a part. They are currently responsible for a formidable range of rules and regulations affecting market structure, pricing behaviour, capital allocation, quality (and sometimes quantity) of inputs, provision of information, safety standards, and so on, many of which are a hangover from the old command and control structure. Internal markets, however, also attract strong arguments for economic and quality regulation, including the generation of the information needed to inform purchasers, the strengthening of the accountability of both purchasers and providers, and the reduction of the transaction costs involved in enforcing standards entirely via contracts.

If the internal market is not to be quickly stifled by regulation, each area of public interest thought potentially to warrant intervention will require strict scrutiny. All proposed regulations might be tested against the following questions:

- Why is intervention necessary?
- Why cannot the outcome be left to the market?
- Will the benefits of intervention outweigh the costs?
- Can adequate control be obtained through purchasers?
- If direct control of providers is needed, is it required for a transition period or in the long term?
- Is it possible to deploy a pro-competitive method of regulation (ie one that is an aid to the operation of competitive markets rather than a substitute for competition) whether this influences market structure or market behaviour?
- For each issue that requires direct regulation of providers, is the timing and method of implementation governed by explicit criteria?

This set of questions rests on the view that the main purpose of regulation is to protect the interests of consumers and others against opportunistic behaviour by providers, while maintaining incentives for efficient performance. The experience of regulation in other fields suggests that this is best achieved by actively promoting the development of contestable markets. The implication is that the central role for regulation should be to improve the structure and working of markets, not to try to mimic their behaviour.

Central policy

A fifth player is the NHS central policy making function. At any time, Ministers can decide to speed up or slow down the development of the market or to shift the balance between line management and market forces. The Tomlinson inquiry indicated that they can also use traditional planning approaches to anticipate the impact of the market and to manage the expected problems of adjustment.[4]

How can a balance be struck between securing competition and meeting the public interests?

The choice implied by this question is false. 'Public interests' are ends, and competition should be seen as a means towards some of these ends, in particular a health service marked by greater efficiency and responsiveness. The question is therefore not about how a balance can be struck between 'competition' and 'public interests' but how can competition be used to promote efficiency and responsiveness without adversely affecting other public interests— for example, improved health, equity, choice, access and patient influence over decisions.

In the new internal market, the main way in which these other public interests can be met is through line management of purchasing. The health service remains publicly financed and district health authorities in their commissioning role remain in a line relationship with the centre. Where the public purpose is not well defined, the greater emphasis of decentralisation leaves it open to purchasers to define different standards (eg on the treatment of varicose veins), which may give rise to problems of equity. But, where public interests are well articulated, purchasers should have the financial clout to ensure that those interests are protected or promoted. Indeed, their incentives to pursue those interests should be stronger than in the previous hierarchical arrangements which sometimes presented health authorities with sharp conflicts of interest. What is more uncertain is whether health authorities have the skills, knowledge and information to protect public interests, but again the clarification of their roles, the recruitment of staff specialising in needs assessment, and the pressure to develop better measures of quality should all have increased rather than reduced their competence in these respects. Comparisons with perfect systems should be avoided—because none exists.

The critical changes introduced by the internal market are the substitution of contractual relationships for hierarchical arrangements, and the trialling of two types of purchasers. Evidence is still coming in on whether and how the various public interests can be as well protected via contractual relationships as through hierarchical arrangements, and on the implications in terms of transaction costs. However, many European countries have successfully protected public interests in the health field through contracts with hospitals not owned by the central government. Critics see the existence of two types of purchasers (or three if the role of local authorities in purchasing community care is taken into account) as more threatening, because of the scope for shifting costs and passing the buck, but where public interests are open to different interpretations and/or the competence of purchasers as agents varies greatly (as is certainly true at present), a plurality of purchasers may paradoxically offer the public greater protection.

One public interest that cannot be adequately met through managing the purchasing side of the market is the government's ownership responsibility for trusts and other public providers. This requires the establishment and monitoring of financial regimes that will ensure public assets are efficiently used.

The benefits of competition are obtained through contestability on the provider side of the market. If provider markets are to be efficient they need to have the following characteristics:

- market structures that are competitive or at least contestable;
- adequate information on price and quality;
- providers that respond to financial signals and can allocate resources in line with market signals;
- financial allocation systems that discourage risk selection.

The prime objective of market regulation should be to create or maintain these conditions.

There is a common assumption that these regulatory functions require the development of special rules and possibly a special regulatory organisation. In New Zealand, it is expected that the normal anticompetitive legislation applying to other sectors of the

economy will be sufficient to maintain competitive behaviour
among the New Zealand equivalents of trusts, the Crown Health
Enterprises. On the other hand, in The Netherlands some com-
mentators believe that the existing national legislation on anticompetitive behaviour and the various European Community Direc-
tives will not be sufficient to prevent abuses of market power in the
health sector. One reason for the initial optimism in New Zealand
may be that the structure of the market has been redesigned from
scratch on both the purchaser and the provider sides with the
deliberate aim of encouraging competition.

References

1. Department of Health. *Working for patients*. London: HMSO, 1989.
2. Department of Health. *Promoting better health*. London: HMSO, 1987.
3. Appleby J *et al. How do we measure competition?* London: National Association of Health Authorities and Trusts, 1991.
4. Tomlinson B. *Report of the inquiry into London's health service, medical
   education and research*. London: HMSO, 1992.
5. Performance figures show variable quality of NHS care. *The Times*,
   April 27, 1993.
6. Editorial. Dicing with death rates. *Lancet* 1993; **341**: 1183–4.
7. Hopkins A, ed. *The role of hospital consultants in clinical directorates*. London: Royal College of Physicians, 1993.
8. Department of Health. *The Health of the Nation*. London: HMSO,
   1992.
9. Department of Health. *The Patient's Charter*. London: HMSO, 1992.
10. Berk M, Monheit AC. The concentration of health expenditures: an
    update. *Health Affairs* 1992; **11**: 145–9.

Editor's suggestions for further reading

Department of Health. *Managing the new NHS*. London: Department of
Health, 1993.
Ham C, Appleby J. *The further direction of the National Health Service*. Birmingham: National Association of Health Authorities and Trusts, 1993.
Institute of Health Services Management Policy Unit. *Future health care
options: final report*. London: Institute of Health Services Management,
1993.
Burson-Marsteller. *The future of UK health care*. London: Burson-Marsteller,
1993.

DISCUSSION

Clive Smee: First, what kind of market do we want? Because of the
uncertainties and constraints on the market so far, I think we could
have almost any kind of market so long as it is a managed or

regulated market. I do not believe anybody seriously considers having a totally free market, so I think it is neither sensible nor profitable to discuss that option. We are talking about options within the broad term of a managed or regulated market.

Secondly, who are the key players in the market? The NHS Management Executive and the Department of Health, including Ministers, appear to have been the key players so far. We now need to consider who they should be in the future.

The key player whose role has to be much further developed is the purchaser. In most markets, the prime purpose of regulation, beyond concern with safety standards, food hygiene and similar matters, is to protect the users who cannot protect their own interests because they face a natural monopoly (hence the creation of Oftel, Ofgas and so on). However, if purchasers can be effective agents for the users of health services, what role, if any, is left for a separate regulatory agency?

Thirdly, how can a balance be struck between competition and meeting the public interest? The word 'balance' suggests the presence of choice, but I believe the choice is only apparent. Competition is a means to an end, not an end in itself, and its opposite is monopoly, not planning—so competition does not rule out planning. The NHS reforms and the internal market were aimed at providing a delivery system better able to meet the public interest than a monopoly provider that, in the government's view, failed to meet it in at least the two important respects of providing incentives for efficiency and a service responsive to its users.

The clinician's role in a managed or regulated market must also be considered. This is absolutely critical in at least two areas: first, clinicians can provide information to help make the market work and, secondly, economists do not believe markets can be effective unless there is a good deal of information available on a range of subjects. Clinicians clearly have a central role in informing the market about the quality, effectiveness and appropriateness of the products or services, and in providing information about new products to purchasers. We need therefore to consider how clinicians can provide better information that encourages better service delivery.

Other questions are how can clinicians help to improve the efficiency, effectiveness and quality of providers, contribute to business plans, contract negotiations and service reviews, and more effectively to audit? My impression is that clinicians play far too small a role in all these areas, except possibly in clinical audit. If providers are to improve their efficiency, effectiveness and quality, the role of clinicians must become central.

Alan Maynard: One issue is equity, mentioned briefly by Clive
Smee. Small-area data show that typically there is poor access to
services where the poor live, so the effect of pricing and contracting on distributional issues needs to be considered. Local monopolies also indulge in pricing behaviour that can redistribute deficits
between purchasers.

Secondly, there is little evidence so far about the effectiveness of
the market in achieving change in its first two years, and no programme of evaluation is in place. The evidence from the USA
shows that health care markets create competition in quality, not
in price—what Reinhart has called a 'medical arms race'—which
creates medical Disneylands. There is little evidence from the USA
that managed competition has been successful either in controlling cost expansion or in improving resource allocation.

Graham Winyard: A dilemma about political accountability and the
market is that Ministers are held accountable for all sorts of issues for
which in a proper market they would not be. A good example is that
of equal opportunities. All providers should follow equal opportunities legislation, but the Department of Health and the NHS Management Executive want to go further and 'interfere' by requiring
providers to appoint specific proportions of female managers, consultants and other staff. There are many such issues in which the centre wants to become involved in the detail of how trusts manage their
affairs. Such intervention does not sit easily with market concepts.

Anthony Hopkins: Clinicians are sensitive to the point about equity
and the distribution of resources, and are aware that the facilities
both in primary and in secondary care are less good in the less
attractive parts of the country. What incentives might be proposed
to redistribute better doctors and better facilities to the economically deprived inner city areas?

Alan Maynard: All sorts of complex incentives work in the internal
market which we do not really understand. Some of the big cities
have regional specialties. These tend to be priced on item-of-ser-
vice, much more carefully priced than the block contracts. There is
some evidence that some inner city university hospitals with
regional specialties are costing their services more accurately, and
consequently raising their prices, which has redistributive effects.
If their prices are manipulated by reducing block contract prices,
the local city purchasers may not be in deficit, with the result that
the deficit will be redistributed to the country areas. We also need
to consider what mechanisms are available to ensure transfer of
resources into primary care if inner city hospitals close, as seems
likely on the basis of the Tomlinson Report.[1]

David Tod: One reason why inner city care has not developed is because of the tradition of single-handed general practitioners in inner cities. Only in the conurbations where there are large group practices has it been possible to develop adequate primary care. Such practices are rare in central London or in the centre of other cities. We need to consider how best to translate a tradition of single-handed doctors operating in isolation into large groups acting efficiently. When a large teaching practice is established in an inner city area, the standard of care for the patients of that practice begins to rise and more equitable access to care results.

Health authorities in inner cities have in the past not been good either at measuring need or in ensuring that the needs they discover are actually being addressed by the providers; for example, large London teaching hospitals may provide high quality secondary and tertiary care, but relatively low quality care for what might be termed 'social medicine' such as geriatric and psychiatric care near to where patients live. Fundholding general practitioners have a detailed knowledge of their patients' needs, from 'the bottom up', and are now a body large enough to assess need. They therefore can press the providers to provide the equity of access and supply of services appropriate for their local population.

If every practice in the country gained control of its own destiny through having its own budget, there would then be competition between fundholders just as there is competition between providers in the secondary sector. It may be better to have approximately half general practitioners fundholding and the other half working in association with health authority management and purchasing. There would then be competition between the health authority acting for the non-fundholding general practitioners and the fundholding general practitioners, which I think is healthy.

John Sully: Some purchasers use the new system to change services. Examples from my own locality include the following:

- half a million pounds' worth of orthopaedic services moved from Brighton to Worthing hospitals because the service offered by the latter was judged to be better;
- when services for sterilisation were put out to tender, one was won by the local community health services, another by the private sector;
- tenders were won by the private sector in competition with the NHS trusts for nursing home beds to replace long-stay elderly beds.

NHS purchasers of continuing care of the elderly, of services for people with learning disabilities and so on will deal a lot with the private sector. There is a need to be clear about what regulation is required in the private sector.

Anthony Hopkins: Both you and Dr Tod have given examples of successful contract making and of driving the market by purchasing, but we must remember that our discussion is not about successful purchasing alone, but also whether there is a need for regulation.

Stuart Dickens: There is now a necklace of district general hospitals around Birmingham which is taking work out of the city. Apart from those decisions legitimately being made by shire county purchasing authorities about the needs of their local population, purchasing decisions are also being made to support new district general hospitals or extended hospitals, partly based on ensuring that appropriate work is fed into local hospitals so that they stay in balance, not just in financial terms but in clinical terms, and are able to provide a broad range of services.

The consequence is that the major acute unit in South Birmingham is losing something like £6–8 million a year. Another effect is that decisions made by purchasers outside the city, based in some cases on supporting local services because those hospitals are in deficit, are often made against natural patient flows. Half a million pounds may be taken from one hospital, only for it to be found subsequently that patient flows have not changed, despite appropriate down-sizing and reconfiguration decisions having been made in support of the need for a balanced budget. Purchasers need to remain credible in the market-place.

Such problems raise questions about how to manage these transitions. If large sums of money are taken from one unit, we need to know the criteria on which that decision is taken, and to consider some appropriate regulatory intervention.

Ian Carruthers: John Sully and Stuart Dickens have both given examples of purchasing having major influences on service provision. On the one hand, a lot of purchasing shifts are being identified and, on the other, a whole set of mechanisms called standby reserves to minimise the effect of those shifts. This mixed thinking raises the issue as to how far people want to go in letting market mechanisms shake out providers. As someone who is in the real world, I agree in theory to the shake-out, but in practice all sorts of local practical and political pressures prevent it. It may be that the stereotype commercial market is inappropriate in a medical setting. Truly unregulated medical markets have never worked anywhere. We have to think about what we want from the market, and tailor the way purchasing and provision are regulated in order to deliver it.

For me, the dilemma is whether we want a market that deals in *health* or in *primary and secondary health care*. Different infrastructures and approaches are needed. A market in health means developing primary care, for which there are several alternative models: for example, the extension of fundholding and the development of provision in general practice.

Richard Thomson: This may be making a false distinction. Within the purpose of the reforms taking place, are we not concerned about the creation of a health care market that delivers health? There will always be other activities parallel to but outside the health care market concerned with influencing the health of our population. However, the final goal of the purchaser–provider interaction is to create a mechanism that will ensure that the health care delivered is better able to produce effective and appropriate care. Some of our efforts over the next year or two need to be concentrated on defining better what is meant by 'appropriate and effective care' in order to be able to shift resources from inappropriate and ineffective care and use better the resources made available within the health care market.

Bruce Campbell: One of the great difficulties in starting a market in health rather than in health care is in injecting the concept of the market economy into such a tight and inflexible system as the NHS. Clinicians do not have much time, their current heavy workload militates against time spent on health rather than disease care, which is one reason why they do not enter with joy into these discussions. Many clinicians feel characteristics of the market will depend on geographical placement. For doctors like Dr Tod, who have a number of hospitals readily available more or less equally convenient for their patients, true competition may exist. This approaches the ethos of a true market. On the other hand, in some parts of the country, hospitals are 30 miles apart. This, admittedly, seems much further to someone with varicose veins than to someone who needs a coronary artery bypass graft, because distances shrink with big procedures.

Purchasers, be they fundholding general practitioners or health districts, will use the implicit threat of market forces to mould the behaviour and practice of their most convenient hospital, so that it no longer has the ethos of a monopoly. They would prefer their patients to go there, but do not want the local hospital to be a monopoly in the sense that it dictates the way things will be done, so they are likely to use the market in a different way: rather than sending many of their patients elsewhere, they will use the implicit threat to do so (and indeed will send the occasional patient) to achieve what they want locally, which is much more convenient for everybody.

Purchasers lack much of the information necessary for the effective commissioning of care. Governments always look at waiting times because the data are easy to collect, but we should be looking at outcomes, and also consider the important aspect of what I call 'style' from the patient's point of view:

- How much contact time does a patient have with the consultant?
- Is he or she nice to the patient?
- Has the patient been kindly dealt with?

When hospitals measure patient satisfaction, the questions are always framed so that they are able to report that 85% of their patients were happy. In trying to measure health gains and outcomes, it is important not to lose sight of measurements of patient satisfaction with treatment.

Zarrina Kurtz: One kind of competition is that between those clinicians trying to sell a market in health and those trying to sell a market in disease care. I have been involved in the specialty review of child health services by the London Implementation Group, an exercise with some elements of market regulation because the group will be making recommendations about the providers who should continue in the London market.[2] However, this is being done in isolation from an adequate examination of primary care in London, which is crucial to the health of Londoners as it is to those in other inner cities. Deprived populations have the poorest health experience, and a significant proportion are not properly linked into primary care services which play a major role in promoting health and preventing disease. Even if they are registered with a general practitioner, many economically deprived people move their place of residence frequently, and do not have continuity or consistency of contact. Many of them use other providers such as the accident and emergency departments.

Peter Coe: This is a big issue for some of us in the inner city areas. Half the babies in Tower Hamlets in East London are admitted through an accident and emergency department in the first six months of life for either respiratory or gastrointestinal disease. There will be a big time lag before improved primary care and environment have overcome these problems.

Until full capitation has been reached, I do not think we will have equity. I manage one of the few London districts (Tower Hamlets) that has a significant capitation loss: £18 million below target, compared with our neighbouring authority, Camden, which is

£25 million above. There are problems of purchasing for equity when the figures are so far apart. The local general practitioners (very few of whom are fundholders) and I believe that money should be moved into mental health, the care of the elderly and primary health care, and attempts made to achieve equitable access not just across localities and communities but between disease groups and care areas. The market has certainly introduced competition into acute services, but has not yet changed the balance of expenditure between acute and other services. In order to enter the market on regional specialties, one local hospital has offloaded its costs on to local acute services, and I am being asked to pay another £12 million to meet last year's acute case-load target. As another example of the problems arising from equitable care, we will be trying to meet international targets for treating renal diseases within about five years. This is an impossible target for most purchasers, certainly for many fundholding general practitioners, unless some agreed priorities are set. This may well mean further activity taken out of local acute services, and possibly a lessening of the rate of increase of the allocation of funds to mental health.

What the local population wants in terms of health care has to be determined. How can it know what it *should* want, what it values, and whose values should be used?

Graham Winyard: We do not know what sort of market we want, but it will help us over time to work out the answer if major decisions that are taken are made as explicit as possible and the assumptions on which they rest clearly defined. Discussion about decisions needs to be more open than it is now: for example, the difficult decision about whether the future well-being of a major London teaching hospital is more important than developing primary and mental health care for the local population. On the basis of that information, we could start to work out the sort of market we want.

David Taylor: The health authorities' commissioners are *par excellence* regulators—resource allocators. This is a bureaucratic resource allocation system, and unless regulation is totally integrated with it, much of its effect will be lost. The real issue is whether we create something more like a real market in the future with more discretion and choice—first, for consumers, secondly, for primary care practitioners and, thirdly, for secondary in relation to tertiary care. The role of commissioners and health authorities would then become more apparent as regulators. Or, for political and job protection reasons, do we continue to create tier upon tier of regulators regulating regulators?

Alan Torbet: If we start from where the market might start, with primary health care—which is the point of access to services for most people—this potentially destroys any view of equity we may have: first, because in inner city areas, general practice still operates in an essentially competitive rather than collaborative way (which is difficult to manage); secondly, because I do not think there is evidence that patients choose quality general practice, but rather tend to be seduced by convenience and local availability. Of what value is the market in this environment?

I was struck by Dr Tod's comment that we are heading towards a 50:50 balance between general practitioner fundholders and non-fundholders, and whether this is a pivotal point at which to take a view on how the market will develop. It is interesting to observe the development of fundholding in Birmingham where there is a proposal, which it is hoped will be supported by the Department, to have a so-called 'multi-fund' co-operative, bringing over 100 general practitioners in the city into about 20 fundholding units.

A large part of the impetus for this proposal has come from an inherent desire of general practitioners (even fundholders) to see an element of stabilisation, indeed of regulation, in the market environment to avoid chaotic individual decision making having an unplanned impact on the provider services. General practitioners also recognise that, to ensure a degree of equity, a set of systems has to be developed that are as relevant to the needs of people in inner cities as to those in leafy suburbia.

One of the key principles of the multi-fund is to cover a range of general practice in terms of size and the nature of the people served. It is interesting that, rather than go down the untrammelled competition route of individual fundholding, these Birmingham general practitioners seem to think that a degree of self regulation would be quite attractive.

References

1. Tomlinson B. *Report of the inquiry into London's health service, medical education and research.* London: HMSO, 1992.
2. London Implementation Group. *Report of an independent review of specialist services in London—child health services.* London: London Implementation Group, 1993.

3 | Regulating the market

Alasdair Liddell
Regional General Manager,
East Anglian Regional Health Authority

Much of the wider debate about the developing National Health
Service (NHS) market is dogged by confusion about the meaning
of words. 'Purchaser', 'market' and 'regulation' are three examples, acquiring a specific meaning in the NHS context but often
misunderstood because of their more general usage. This is particularly true of 'regulation', which is one person's management and
another person's interference. It often connotes rules, bureaucracy and constraint, although regulation can operate positively
to stimulate change and innovation, for example when used to
promote competition.

Participants in the NHS market are having to learn about regulation as they go. There is as yet no body of precedent to draw on,
and indeed the learning process was hampered by lack of official
acknowledgement that regulation was either legitimate or necessary (*Managing the New NHS*).[1] There may be a substantial body
of literature about market regulation generally, but it is not safe
to transpose this wholesale to the NHS, for the NHS market has
some special characteristics that make it different from the general
case.

Why should there be regulation? This question must be asked
every time any regulatory intervention is considered, because
there are great dangers that the market might be overmanaged,
but the general case for regulation of the NHS market rests on the
view that it cannot be guaranteed that purchasers and providers,
left to their own devices, will *always* act in the public interest.

In this chapter, a framework is offered for exploring regulation
in the NHS market—the potential mechanisms and regulators,
and the kind of interventions that might be made. A distinction is
drawn between management oversight of purchasers and
providers, and regulation of the market in which they participate.

There are three different kinds of relationship between purchasers, providers and the intermediate tier (Fig. 1):

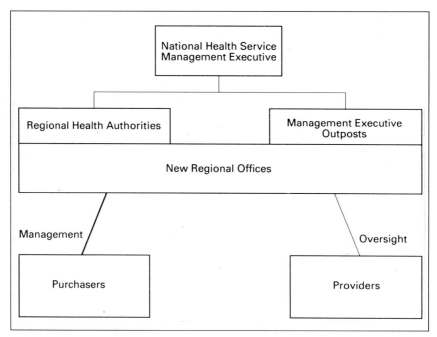

Fig. 1. *The relationship between the NHS Management Executive, the intermediate level, and purchasers and providers. The structure outlined in* Managing the New NHS[1] *shows how regional health authorities and Management Executive 'outposts' will be replaced by eight Regional Offices.*

- *management* of purchasers: essentially a line management relationship to ensure that purchasers are effective in identifying and meeting the health needs of their population;
- *oversight* of providers: again a line management relationship to ensure viability and financial performance of NHS trusts;
- *regulation* of the market: actual or potential intervention directed either to purchasers or providers or the interactions between them, to ensure that the market works in the public interest. Regulation may be by the intermediate tier, the centre or external regulatory agencies.

The 'oversight' arrow to the provider is thinner than the 'management' arrow to the purchaser, reflecting our interest in regulation that has a 'light touch', and the fact that providers are also accountable through contracts. A distinction is made between line management activities of the purchaser and oversight of providers, ensuring that they meet necessary financial requirements.* The Secretary of

---

Editor's note: Para 38 of *Managing the New NHS* makes it clear that the NHS Management Executive will manage performance of both purchasers and providers.

State is the ultimate owner of NHS trusts, so the regional offices will be interested in ensuring financial viability. The NHS is not particularly interested in the financial viability or the return on assets of private providers, which are matters for their shareholders.

The question of how the public interest should be defined sets the framework for the whole operation of the market, including regulation. An attempt to regulate a market without an explicit definition of the public interest is likely to result in confused market participants and an increased need for intervention. Table 1

Table 1. Characteristics of the new health system: definition of terms.

Purpose
The purpose of the NHS is to improve the health of the population through health promotion and the provision of treatment and care targeted effectively to meet local needs, and to provide a quality service to individual patients and carers.

Values
The pursuit of this purpose requires a system of accountability that reflects outcomes, rather than merely inputs or outputs. These outcomes are based on a series of values that reflect both the needs of the individual consumer and benefits to the population as a whole:

Equity	There should be a comprehensive approach to assessing need, and equal treatment for equal need.
Access	Everyone should be able to obtain services when and where they are needed.
Efficiency	Services should achieve intended quality for the most economic use of resources.
Appropriateness	While relevant to need, patterns and delivery of service will accord with current standards. They will balance best professional practice, ethical codes and government policy with sensitivity to individual and community preferences.
Effectiveness	Services should achieve the best possible health benefit from programmes of prevention, care and treatment.
Responsiveness	The extent and style of services should reflect the reasonable expectations of the population and should allow for choice.

In this context, 'services' denotes the full range of NHS activity, covering health promotion, prevention and diagnosis of illness and disability, and treatment, rehabilitation and continuing care.

Imperatives
These values complement the existing imperatives in the public system (ie effective policy implementation, public accountability and control of public expenditure). Together they form a wide set of objectives which have to be reconciled in many health systems.

suggests an appropriate definition, agreed by the NHS Management Executive and regional general managers in May 1992 as a
statement of the purpose and values of the NHS, subsequently
refined in my own region.[2]

Management of purchasers

The role of a purchasing authority is to identify the health needs
of its population, and to secure services to meet those needs. Purchasers are also expected to work intersectorally with other agencies, to agree a common programme of action to address health
needs across a broader front than health care. To reflect these
broader needs for action, we increasingly refer to 'commissioning'
rather than 'purchasing' of health care. Commissioning authorities are increasingly judged on the *results* they achieve, based on
measures of output and outcome. In accordance with current per-
ceptions of good management practice, the emphasis is on *what* is
achieved, rather than *how*. The market is a mechanism, a means of
securing results.

The principal concern in managing purchasers, therefore, is setting a direction for them and ensuring they achieve it, not in defining *how* the result should be achieved. It is true that, in the event
of failure, the manager of purchasers may be asked to explain how
he or she set about achieving the intended result, but only in terms
of assessing how effectively the mechanism of the market is being
used rather than assessing the effectiveness of the mechanism
itself.

Regional health authorities (and, in future, regional offices) act
as managers of purchasers. Their main roles in this capacity are:

- *setting direction:* setting the strategic context for health and health
  care, identifying the main health priorities, and ensuring proper
  co-ordination between district health authorities, family health
  service authorities (soon to be merged), and fundholding general
  practitioners.
- *allocating resources:* allocating revenue funding through the
  weighted capitation formula for district health authorities, and
  allocation policies for family health service authorities and fundholding general practitioners.
- *managing performance:* negotiating objectives that reflect both
  national and local concerns, and which are demanding but
  achievable, monitoring results, and securing improved performance through challenge, development and sanction.

Oversight of providers

A key feature of the NHS reforms is the devolution of management responsibility. The establishment of NHS trusts is a prime
example of this policy. Given substantial new freedoms, they are
intended to exercise substantial autonomy over *how* they achieve
their objectives, being held to account for *what* they agree with
purchasers through service contracts. NHS trusts, however, still
remain part of the NHS, formally accountable to the Secretary of
State. They should also:

- provide services to purchasers' specifications, meeting both
  quality and cost targets;
- contribute views and information to help commissioners
  develop effective strategies;
- submit business plans for approval;
- achieve a 6% return on capital assets;
- break even financially;
- remain within their agreed external financing limit;
- demonstrate value for money.

These requirements are concerned with the effective function-
ing of the provider as an organisation, not with the effective operation of the market. These are the kind of requirements with
which any owner would be concerned, and have nothing to do
with market regulation. This oversight role is currently performed by 'outposts' of the NHS Management Executive, but
soon will fall within the remit of regional offices. Doubtless any
private sector participant in the NHS also has to demonstrate similar financial and business viability to its owners or shareholders.

There are other requirements which are more difficult to distinguish from regulation and which cause particular problems. These
are policy requirements which have emerged during the
implementation of the market, without it always being clear precisely what is expected, and who is to ensure compliance. They
include:

- responsibility for training;
- work towards 'Opportunity 2000';
- establishing appropriate working hours for junior doctors;
- saving energy;
- healthy workplace initiatives;
- restraining pay according to government policy.

To the extent that these requirements reflect the values of the
NHS, they can probably be defined as *ownership* requirements, ie

expectations placed on providers by virtue of their membership of the NHS. Arguably, a good test is to question which of these requirements are placed on *all* (provider) participants of the market. Those that are so placed could be described as 'regulation', while those placed only on NHS participants reflect 'ownership'. On this test, the above are all 'ownership' requirements, reflecting membership of the NHS.

Regulation

The first part of this chapter has described the management of purchasers and the oversight of providers. Anything else can be described as market regulation. Sometimes regulation is of providers, and sometimes of purchasers, sometimes it governs the interactions between them. There are three main types of regulatory intervention:

- *setting the rules of the market:* for example, the requirements that those general practitioners who become fundholding have at least a certain number of patients; that contracts be signed by 1st April; that certain minimum sets of data be provided; that invoices be settled within a specified time period—and so on;
- *resolving disputes:* conciliation and arbitration to resolve disputes about contracting, terms of performance, or alleged breaches of the market rules;
- *adjusting incentives:* intervening in the market to adjust incentives to alter market behaviour in some desirable way; for example, the approval of a merger between purchasing authorities; the refusal to approve a merger between trusts (to maintain or increase purchaser leverage); the allocation of capital, or earmarked revenue resources; decisions to underwrite the costs of market exits, in order to ensure that change resulting from market activity is appropriately managed.

These mechanisms highlight two particular features of regulation. First, regulation requires *judgement*. Deciding when and how to intervene with a new rule or an adjusted incentive, or when a merger may or may not be in the public interest, are not matters which can be prescribed by a strict set of rules, but they require insight and experience, often best informed by local knowledge. Secondly, regulation is not just an imposition from above. The market participants themselves will often seek a regulatory intervention to resolve a dispute, or what they perceive to be a failure of the market to operate effectively in their area of interest.

Who are the regulators?

There are, first, a number of *external regulatory agencies*, including:

- the local authorities (concerned with, for example, environmental health, fire prevention and pollution control);
- the Health and Safety Executive (concerned with health and safety);
- the Audit Commission (concerned with financial probity);
- the Royal Colleges (concerned with postgraduate training and continuing medical education).

The NHS should arguably rely on these external agencies, and not seek to duplicate or pre-empt their function.

The *centre*, represented by the Government (through legislation), Ministers (through their statutory powers), and the NHS Management Executive, has a significant regulatory role. The influence of the centre is on a national scale, so it tends to regulate in a rather formal way, by establishing rules for general application, but there are other specific examples, such as decisions on mergers of trusts or health authorities. The intervention can sometimes be relatively informal, such as a letter from the Chief Executive of the NHS, urging that urgent cases should not be deferred admission on financial grounds.

Regional health authorities have also regulated the market within their region, usually in more informal ways. Thus, many regional health authorities have established 'contracting principles' which apply to the interaction between purchasers and providers and represent criteria for intervention. Most of them have established a business cycle, with deadlines for the issue of prices and the signing of contracts, usually within the framework of the national cycle.

Regional health authorities also have acted as the agents of the centre in ensuring compliance with national rules. They have been in a good position to do so, with a greater detail of local knowledge both of circumstances and of participants. This local knowledge has often enabled them to judge when it was *not* appropriate to intervene. Regional health authorities also have had a part to play in promoting and assessing the competence of bids for NHS trust status, and in influencing decisions about the structure of the market through organisational change.

Perhaps one of the more significant examples so far of regulation by regional health authorities has been the management of the pace of change—usually to slow the rate of market exit. Typically, the market signals that a particular hospital is uncompetitive through the withdrawal of some contracts, and prices for the remaining workload have to increase, because there is a smaller base against which overheads may be set. This can lead to a rapid spiral towards closure, unless these additional costs can be underwritten in the short term to allow the necessary actions to reduce overhead costs to be taken in a planned way. This kind of intervention requires specific local knowledge.

Management Executive outposts, although primarily concerned with the oversight of providers have also taken part in certain regulatory activities, having played an important role in judging the competence of applications for NHS trust status, and any mergers, and in resolving any disputes.

Editor's note

In his original manuscript, Alasdair Liddell went on to stress how the existence of two local regulatory bodies (the regional health authorities and the Management Executive outposts), in addition to the Management Executive itself and external regulators, emphasised the need for clarity about who was responsible for what. Presumably this was one of the aspects of the NHS considered by the Functions and Manpower Review, chaired by Kate Jenkins, and one of the considerations that led the Secretary of State to simplify the structure of the NHS, as illustrated in Figs. 2–4. In Fig. 3, it is clear how local strategic development and purchasing, and the provision of health and health care services are subject both to performance management and market regulation.

Acknowledgements

This chapter has drawn upon a number of internal discussion papers, including the following:
Jarrold K, *et al. The local expression of central management.* 2 June 1992.
Kemp P. *The nature and purpose of regulation in National Health Service markets.* Economics and Operational Research Division. July 1992.
Langlands A. *Characteristics of the new health system: regulatory framework.* 2 June 1992.
Spry C. *The intermediate tier and the emerging strategic agenda.* 17 February 1993.
Thornton S. *What is market regulation?* 14 June 1992.

References

1. *Managing the New NHS.* London: Department of Health, 1993.
2. Seven steps to better health and health services. Cambridge: East Anglian Regional Health Authority, 1993.

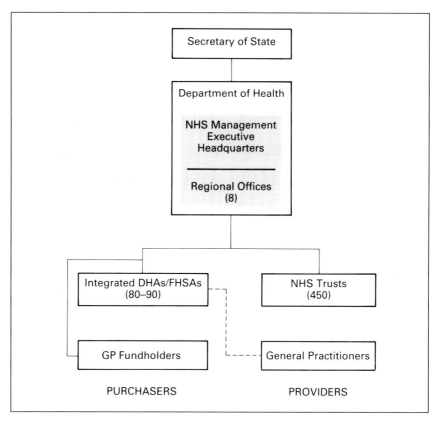

Fig. 2. *New structure of the NHS*

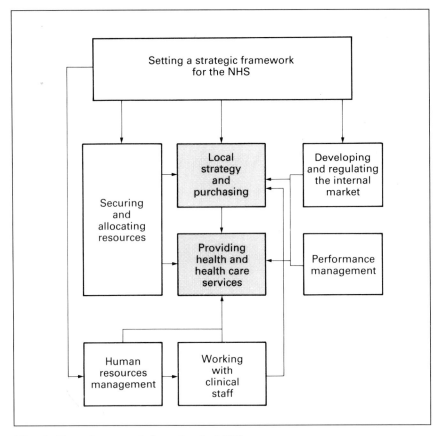

Fig. 3. *Functions carried out in the NHS*

Wider Department of Health

- Advising Ministers
- Formulating health policy
- Public health
- Family Health Services (exc. General Medical Services)
- Personal social services (including children)
- Managing relationship with rest of Government
- International relations
- Managing relationship with other agencies and statutory bodies

NHSME (Headquarters)

- Setting NHS Strategic Framework;
  - *Assessing health needs*
  - *Research and development*
  - *Formulating operational policy*
- Securing and allocating resources
- Human resources management
- Working with clinical staff
- Performance management
- Developing and regulating the internal market
- Managing General Medical Services
- Supporting Ministers

NHSME (Regional offices)

- Ensuring compliance with the regulatory framework for the internal market
- Managing performance of purchasers and providers
- Disputes arbitration
- Approving GPFH application and budgets
- Purchaser development
- Targeted contribution to central work on policy and resources

Purchasers (DHA/FHSA)

- Setting purchasing strategy – targeted to meet local needs
- Purchasing services in accordance with local strategy
- Ensuring delivery to quality and cost targets in contracts
- Primary Care Development
- Administration of GPs' (& dentists, opticians and pharmacists) terms of service
- Patient Registration

Providers

- Providing services to purchasers' specifications
- Managing delivery to quality and cost targets in contracts
- Meeting the terms of the 'established order' and mandatory financial duties
- Meeting purchaser and NHSME VFM targets
- Contributing views and information to local strategy

Fig. 4. *Allocation of main functions to the new structure of the NHS*

4 | A purchaser's perspective on regulating the market in health care

Ian Carruthers
Chief Executive, Dorset Health Commission

Competition for its own sake is not always appropriate, but managed competition should be created and supported where it improves both the services to the users of health services and value for money. Managed markets should be used to bring about desirable change. Many would argue that regulation is an activity which purchasers undertake across the range of their providers, which is undoubtedly so in some circumstances. Such regulation by purchasers applies to the ideal market-place, and to the normal transactions of contracting between purchasers and providers, usually undertaken in a local geographic area. The role of any intermediate level of management is to regulate across markets in this sense and to manage the total market-place to meet national priorities for health care. The development of different models of regulation should be encouraged, as this will advance our knowledge and practice to secure the best possible way forward for the future.

Agenda for the managed market

The outcomes to be achieved through the managed market centre on:

- improved health outcomes;
- increased output;
- changes in working practices and service patterns as movement to day-case and increased outpatient work proceeds;
- provision of more local services, which may involve the localisation of those hitherto considered as regional services, provided that professional standards and quality can be maintained;
- reduced waiting times;
- removal of inefficiencies in services associated with embedded professional habits, organisational structures, bureaucratic or legal rules or under- and over-funding of staff and facilities. Examples include the avoidance of unnecessary hospital admissions,

excessive lengths of stay, blocked or unused beds, and the use of medical procedures not of proven cost effectiveness;
- greater accountability for clinical work;
- greater professional and managerial freedoms;
- better development of self care;
- creation of strategies which facilitate the attainments by purchasers and providers of the targets outlined in *The Health of the Nation*[1] and in *The Patient's Charter*;[2]
- successful implementation of *Caring for people*[3] through well established jointly commissioned and funded strategies which reshape the provision of continuing care both in hospitals and in the nursing home sector;
- increasing the influence of the consumer (by which is meant general practitioners and patients) on the commissioning strategy of the district health authority;
- shifting resources to achieve a balance between primary and secondary care so that primary care becomes the principal focus for health. This can be facilitated by involving general practice more centrally in management, especially as practices develop their provider role by directly managing district nurses, health visitors and other health professionals;
- creating a 'performance culture' in primary and secondary care, designed to secure responsiveness to the users of health services, higher quality standards and value for money;
- developing and reshaping general practices, hospitals and community health service providers to meet the future needs of the population;
- improving the effectiveness and performance of purchasers, whether they be family health services authorities, district health authorities or fundholding general practitioners;
- establishing local alliances to improve health, through engaging with a network of organisations outside the National Health Service (NHS), such as local authorities, chambers of commerce and local employers, all of which can in different ways affect the health of the local population.

Conditions necessary to develop the managed market

Clive Smee showed in Chapter 2 how the internal market in the NHS does not possess all the characteristics of a commercial market. However, managers and others must create the conditions which secure the benefits that flow from a market culture. These include the development of effective purchasers and strong providers, the creation and utilisation of mechanisms to secure change, rules to facilitate day-to-day operation of the market, and the development of market regulation.

Development of effective purchasers

The role of the purchaser is to identify the health needs of the population for which it is responsible and to ensure that contracts are placed with providers to supply the services to meet them. Purchasers will need to display a range of attributes if they are to make a difference to health. They need to:

- have a clear vision of the health care requirements to meet the needs of their population;
- have power to effect change through contract negotiations;
- be close to and empowered by their consumers, namely, the patients and general practitioners;
- create the right financial environment and management culture to facilitate the reshaping of services, often in difficult circumstances;
- provide incentives to act efficiently and responsively, frequently in the face of resistance from local providers.

All this requires purchasers to have information on market prices, the availability of suppliers and the range of services provided.

Many of these attributes are applicable both to fundholding general practitioners and to district health authorities, and may entail the reconfiguration of health authority purchasers into larger units so that scarce skills can be best used, and in order to provide more leverage for change. Competition and collaboration between fundholders, whose actions focus on individuals, and district health authorities, which are responsible for total populations, are providing incentives to change. The development of purchasers is necessary to secure the benefits of the market.

Development of strong providers

Strong providers must be developed if the market is to function effectively. The process of gaining NHS trust status enables each organisation to take stock of its activities and improve its capability for dealing with the challenges with which it will be confronted. Attaining NHS trust status is the beginning, rather than the end, of the process. The formation of a trust is merely one means of securing better delivery of health care for the population to be served.

NHS trusts expect to supply more customer-focused services and treat more patients, yet remain financially viable. They must utilise their new freedoms, and create and reward strategies which introduce changed working practices, so that consumer-orientated services, improvements to information, and high quality care can be developed within the available resources provided through their contracts. This will require a new cultural approach, clear vision, creative programmes of personal and organisational development, a sense of ownership by key staff groups of the direction in which the trust is going, high standards of leadership and a financial framework to manage such transitions as may be necessary. Clinicians need to be at the heart of managerial activity so that local services continue to grow and develop.

Creation of mechanisms to secure desirable change in the managed market

Purchasers and providers must work together and create mechanisms for delivering change in an appropriate and planned way.

Clear messages need to be conveyed from the Department of Health and the NHS Management Executive as to whether provider or purchaser failure will be allowed. For the first two years of the reformed health service, purchasers were encouraged to support a 'steady state', and standby reserves were created to protect providers, particularly in inner London, from the full consequences of the market. The implementation of the Tomlinson Report[4] is likely to result in the closure of some providers, but these must be planned with care so as to maintain services to communities.

A framework is needed for managing the entry and exit of providers to and from the market. This must include financial strategies to manage the transition, and relocation packages to redistribute key staff groups to areas of need. Providers need to have stable financial frameworks in order to reshape their activities and time to manage change. Incentives need to be created by purchasers to facilitate provider change. This is crucial to achieving the benefits that the market can offer. Competition needs to be created: it does not just happen. Purchasers have a key role in encouraging the entry of new providers where this is appropriate. They should:

- supply public information on contracts, including prices and quality issues;
- consider placing some contracts with the private sector;

- develop tendering for services;
- create new managed units as well as reshape existing units, but these must be floated off to independence, such as trust status, within a defined time;
- prime new suppliers by underwriting costs through the allocation of capital and longer-term service contracts;
- encourage the entry of new managements which are prepared to manage the existing facilities more effectively;
- encourage the development of new role and service models for others to build upon, particularly reflecting local consumer choice.

Regulation may be needed to ensure that purchasers and providers do not create static efficiency, engage in hostile unplanned take-overs, impair research and development and professional training, and stifle the taking of longer-term risks that stand a realistic chance of improving services.

It is important to recognise that competition with the private sector is limited because in most instances the price of the private sector is greater, and is unlikely to occur in the long run until prices converge. Given the low prices of the public sector and the drive for better value for money, productivity and efficiency, the narrowing of the price gap is likely only if the private sector reduces its prices, which seems unlikely (not least because many private providers operate on a for-profit basis). Competition between private and public sector providers is unlikely to increase unless there are marked variations in access time. As the same labour force of clinicians is used in both areas, this is not easy to achieve.

More sophisticated techniques for contracting need to be developed, as do clear purchasing strategies which provide long-term direction. Purchasers and providers must work together. This will minimise the risks of unplanned change and is more likely to bring about major benefits to local communities.

Stronger and different purchasers are likely to emerge as a result of mergers of district health authorities, the increase in the numbers of fundholding practices, and the move to commissioning primary and secondary care through joint working between district health authorities, family health services authorities and local authorities.

Users of health services should be empowered through *The Patient's Charter*[2] to exercise their rights. Their choices will influence the market in the long run. Information about services and outcomes should be more readily available, and consumer groups have greater prominence in shaping the nature, range and scale of services commissioned.

For any market to work well, all participants must have access to accurate and timely information. The information presently available reflects the need of an administered organisation: changes are needed if there is to be a shift to a market base. Hitherto, there has been little need to develop patient-based data, but billing and invoicing will change this. The need for individual patient costing to recoup income will require better information for a more developed market approach. Contracting is a driving force in achieving this change, but organisations also need better information to become more efficient. Open information is also important in promoting competition; the requirement for all contracts to be public will in itself increase competition in key areas. A 'commercial in-confidence' approach to information is not appropriate in a public, state-controlled health service.

Incentives for purchaser and provider are essential to encourage competition. For the purchaser, efficient behaviour will be promoted by targets set from above, management controls and public pressure. Good performance will be rewarded and poor performance managed through the accountability process, through which the intermediate level of management review purchasers on behalf of the NHS Management Executive. Purchasers need to develop competence to negotiate with providers efficiently. Contracts set explicit targets for providers, each of whom will wish to perform better than other suppliers. All this will promote competition, but care must be taken to ensure that providers do not dominate purchasers, or vice versa, as a balanced set of relationships and power is likely to bring out the best from both.

Operating the managed market

The NHS has several different types of market:

- highly competitive markets such as in London and in other major cities in which there may be overcapacity of provision;
- markets driven by custom and practice in which referral patterns from general practitioners are stable and unlikely to change;
- markets in which there is one dominant provider and no alternatives within a reasonable geographic distance;
- markets in which several providers exist but are reluctant to compete. In this situation, healthy tensions may need to be created so that there is impetus to improvement of care;

- market areas in which it may be inefficient to encourage competition; for example, some regional services such as forensic psychiatry.

Each of these situations has to be developed and managed so that health service delivery is maximised for the benefit of the population.

How should the market operate?

If it is accepted that we are operating in a managed market, it needs to be made clear that all participants must play by the same rules if the best health and the best value health care for communities are to be achieved. The following guiding principles (intended to be illustrative rather than comprehensive and prescriptive) may be suggested, within which purchasers and providers alike could operate:

- the existing rights to free NHS diagnosis, treatment and care, including extracontractual and tertiary referrals, should be facilitated and not constrained by the contracting process;
- existing referral procedures and practices should continue: these are the continued right of self referral to accident and emergency services, referral by general practitioner to a hospital consultant, and tertiary referral from one hospital consultant to another;
- priority for treatment should be based upon the clinical judgement of relative patient need. However, priorities need to be constrained within the context of agreed waiting times outlined in *The Patient's Charter*[2] and in contracts between purchaser and provider;
- the objectives of purchasers should be to negotiate contracts with providers that offer the best range of services for their residents, balancing considerations of local access and quality with competing priorities for available resources;
- the objective of providers should be to deliver the services as specified in the contract, including open access to information about performance against the contract. In some instances, it may be appropriate to have a code of conduct or practice between purchaser and provider on the supply and use of information;
- contracts should be drawn up on the basis of mutual trust and collaboration. Antagonism in contract negotiations is not in the best interest of patient, purchaser or provider. Clear agreement on core values and principles underpinning the delivery of health services will enhance their quality;

- purchasers and providers have a responsibility to avoid agreeing terms of contracts that would impede consultants and other health professionals in exercising responsible clinical judgement about the treatment of individual patients;
- each purchasing contract should be part of a coherent purchasing plan compatible with the purchasing strategies of other relevant purchasers and reflect national and regional policies and priorities;
- long-term understandings between purchaser and providers or between groups of purchasers or providers should be encouraged, where such understandings can provide stability to protect services at a vulnerable stage of growth or to enable a more effective use of limited resources;
- programmes to reduce costs and increase productivity should be addressed as part of the contracting exercise and not imposed through unreasonable purchasing decisions. It is not in the purchaser's long-term interest to drive costs down and put pressure on the provider so that service continuity is threatened without well planned alternatives being available;
- purchasers should be able to demonstrate rationality, objectivity and responsiveness in their contracting decisions, and must avoid making decisions which merely protect the interests of a particular health care provider;
- the NHS is part of the public sector of the UK, and the normal rules of priority and conduct should apply. Gamesmanship is neither synonymous with good management nor in the best interests of patients or services. Purchasing discussions should be honest: it is unacceptable to play off providers by misrepresenting purchasing intentions;
- there should be no unfair competition through collusion between units or purchasers, through rigging of prices between cartels of providers or purchasers, or between purchasers and providers;
- providers should not exploit their position as monopoly suppliers to a major purchaser. Such exploitation may protect the provider but will usually militate against the total needs of the population being met, as the source, to meet the monopoly provider's demands, will have negative effects on health and health service delivery;
- purchasers and providers should adopt responsible marketing policies, so that public expectations are not unrealistically raised in order to place pressure on purchasers and providers;
- purchasers should not seek to depress their capacity to

commission health care by holding contingency funds that are unrealistically large;

- monitoring should be a genuine attempt to improve value for money, not a game of cops and robbers where purchasers are trying to catch providers or vice versa.

Role of the intermediate level of management in market regulation

Regional offices must develop a role as overseer and moderator of the market to ensure both that individual purchasing strategies are compatible with the health needs of the entire population of the region and also that the trusts continue to operate in a responsible way within the NHS.

The health care market is complex. Short-term gain or local benefit can have a devastating impact on the long-term or wider provision of health services to the population as a whole. The market cannot be viewed as affecting only any one local fundholding practice, district health authority or family health services authority. Decisions made by one purchaser may well have an impact beyond its resident population on to neighbouring districts, or across the region. For example, the decision by one purchaser to pull out of a service funded jointly by three or four purchasers may well make the service non-viable for all of them.

This is where the regional offices and the Management Executive have a major role to play. The intermediate tier is in an ideal position within the hierarchy of the health service to influence and deliver the benefits of the market, and, as neither purchaser nor provider, to act as an objective manager of the market. It can, and must, appraise the progress being made by purchasers and providers, and should also have a clear vision of the benefits that the market can bring to the health of the region's population.

Regulation should take place only when the natural interactions between purchaser and provider work against the achievement of national priorities for improving health care. Interventions must therefore be limited. Any regulatory framework should facilitate market management without stifling innovation, by defining clear market operating rules and by being sufficiently flexible to manage change across different market-places and structures through a style which is both light in touch and encourages issues to be resolved in the local market-place between purchaser and provider. Regulation or intervention should not necessarily result from protests from those on the unfortunate end of change, but may be through incentives and penalties exercised in response to the behaviour of purchasers or providers, or by controlling the entry and exit of purchasers and providers, to ensure that balanced power exists to deliver the national priorities for health.

Ways of minimising the need for regulation include the development of a common language for contracting, the definition of financial standards, and the exchange of information. Regulation should help develop purchaser and provider performance simultaneously: the dominance of one is likely to lead to the underperformance of the other.

The lessons so far

Only limited experience has been gained of the managed market, but the lessons so far include the following:

- the underlying values of the reformed NHS facilitate the use of the market to achieve change;
- the NHS market is expected to behave differently from other markets, and benefits can best be achieved if a managed market is developed;
- each purchaser needs to be clear about the outcomes to be achieved before using the market as a mechanism for change;
- competition for its own sake is not always appropriate, but managed competition should be created and the market used only where it improves the services available and the value for money;
- there is a range of individual markets, for each of which the behaviour required to secure change is different;
- competition with the private sector is likely to be marginal until prices converge. In the short term, activity will focus on an internal managed market;
- better ways are needed of facilitating entry to and exit from the managed market;
- national personnel policies are needed for the relocation of key individuals, so that scarce skills are retained within the NHS;
- mechanisms to secure change are limited. More needs to be done to secure consumer choice and encourage the users of health services to press for change;
- embedded inefficiencies can be tackled only by changing professional habits, organisation, and reducing bureaucracy. It is important to focus on effectiveness, outcomes of interventions, changes in clinical practice, and attitudinal changes in terms of the ownership of resources. Foundations need to be built for the long term. Purchasers using the managed market must balance long-term direction with short-term expediency;

- the evidence is weak for achieving greater efficiency or value for money in medicine from competition. The managed market will help purchasers and providers reshape their priorities, but chronic underfunding is unlikely to be resolved without a change in national priorities, determined by elected government;
- the managed market may have only a limited impact on *health*, as opposed to health care. Other mechanisms are needed to promote health and prevent disease. The market therefore has the improvement of delivery of health *services* as its prime focus;
- imperfections in infrastructure exist: these include the difficulty in defining the service available, the lack of and manipulation of information as purchasers and providers exchange and interpret it, and the complexity of understanding quality in all its parameters;
- new ways of acting now occur. There is secrecy, cost shifting, accountability as an end rather than a means, an ethos of commercialism detracting from an ethos of service, and inappropriate relationships between purchasers and providers and between managers and clinicians which do not recognise their interdependence and common aims. Evidence from other fields suggests that these are phases commonly moved through before relationships, stability and productive facilitation of change are agreed;
- the transaction costs of the managed market need to be minimised, as it is unacceptable for provider failures to stay around, and inefficiency to be encouraged. The allocation of standby reserves and lack of clarity on whether provider failure will be allowed are creating these circumstances in some areas;
- finally, regulation must ensure that the market does not place too much emphasis on cost, at the risk of diminishing the quality of care provided.

References

1. Department of Health. *The Health of the Nation—a strategy for health in England.* London: HMSO, 1992.
2. Department of Health. *The Patient's Charter.* London: HMSO, 1991.
3. Department of Health. *Caring for people: community care in the next decade and beyond.* London: HMSO, 1989.

DISCUSSION

Ian Carruthers: Strong purchasers and providers are needed, and their relative roles considered. Individual providers deliver care through people within their organisation. Purchasers define health needs and ensure health services are delivered. They have the responsibility for meeting local health needs, and must therefore be managers of the total health care system so that services are delivered through providers in a way that produces a balance between primary, community and secondary care and a wider health agenda. Purchasers need clear messages about what is and is not acceptable. They are sometimes the true regulators, but cannot regulate when they are one of a number of purchasers. Furthermore, competition implies tendering, and often short-term perspectives. There is a need to consider how purchasers and providers can work together collaboratively over the long term to enable change to be achieved in a way acceptable to all, that is appropriate and not destructive of good services already in existence.

Our best results in achieving change have been when clinicians have been actively involved in making the decisions. However, clinical directorates are sometimes a mechanism for provider managers to abrogate their responsibilities for strong central management of their organisations. The major fear is that we should not be over-regulated.

Anthony Hopkins: Ian Carruthers has underlined the need both to educate and to strengthen the skills of purchasers, and to strengthen the management skills of providers and clinicians to achieve change. He outlines a potentially useful definition of regulation as being to reorganise the necessary limitations of competition in health care and to develop a framework to secure the maximum benefits. To consider how best to do this is the subject of this book.

David Johnson: We need to remember that we are at the early stages in the development of a radical change in the organisation of the NHS, and to be wary of raising our expectations too high and of drawing too early conclusions about what is being achieved. Chapters 3 and 4 both underline the need for more clarity about what actions are appropriate in making progress now. There is a good deal of nervousness about whether people are taking the right actions, whether they are in purchasing or providing care. However, if in a year from now we are still talking about a lack of evidence of what is being achieved by the introduction of a market that will then be three years old, the question will arise as to whether the changes should continue. The service should take stock this year by collecting good and bad examples of the tensions introduced by the internal market—examples of where change has worked to the benefit of patients, or may have worked against their interests.

I support the need for some form of regulation, and would be comfortable with regulation of providers, as well as a stronger line management function for purchasers. However, there is a need to reshape the intermediate level of management. Most providers would say that the concentration on core performance measures of trusts by the present Management Executive outposts has been with a 'light touch' (to use Alasdair Liddell's phrase). This has been welcomed, and such regulation is working. It has not been the style, however, that most health regions have used in the past. We delude ourselves if we pretend that other potential regulators have moved away from that old bureaucratic style.

If the intermediate tier is to be the regulator of what is in the public interest in the future, more thought needs to be given to its structure: who will make those decisions, who will advise, and in what sort of context will those decisions be made?

Finally, I would be concerned if involving clinicians in dialogue with purchasers was seen as an abrogation of the management responsibilities of any provider. The appropriateness of clinical involvement is to engage clinicians in a dialogue about service provision and contracts, not to hand over to them the negotiation and agreement of contracts.

Sir William Doughty: As chairman of a regional health authority, I might be expected to be in favour of returning to the old regime, but that is not my position. I believe in the market, but we need to look at what *cannot* be managed by the market. Its impact needs to be watched over, and to some extent controlled—but, as already stated, such regulation has to be by a 'light touch'.

The relationship between providers and purchasers must be based on openness and understanding. Marks and Spencer discovered a long time ago that collaboration with providers is beneficial: any organisation that tries to put its suppliers out of business will not get on very well. Purchasers have to try to understand the problems of the providers as well as those they themselves are trying to resolve.* Data act as the lubricant between purchasers and providers. Purchasers need information in order to place contracts properly. We are a long way from establishing good outcomes and real measurement of quality. We all know how difficult it is to obtain and disseminate good information, but this is essential in the smooth running of any market.

Peter Shrigley: Clinicians were initially diverted from the potential realities of the market by the complexities of the restructuring

---

**Editor's note:* This theme was developed in a series of speeches on purchasing by the Minister of State for Health, Dr Brian Mawhinney, after the workshop.

process and by the relative protection afforded by block contracts. Last Christmas, some consultants sent Christmas cards to some general practitioners, which is an acknowledgement that general practitioners are the driving force behind purchasing. Clinicians are now much more interested in the contracting process, and are willing to talk seriously about changing the shape and nature of some of the services they provide, in line with some of the expressed wishes of purchasers, whether fundholding general practitioners or the district health authority. But they are beginning to ask what are their incentives if they are to be more than merely survival.

Martin Buxton: Purchasers may regulate themselves because they see a responsibility beyond their direct role and because they believe that if they do not regulate themselves, others will. The medical profession will recognise this model of self-regulation, but I do not think we should see purchasers as regulators.

Anthony Hopkins: Purchasers cannot themselves be regulators because they act in the market. Perhaps that single sentence makes clear the need for some sort of additional regulation. If there is to be competition by which we hope to achieve greater efficiency in health care, better and greater responsiveness to the wishes of users and so on, there has to be competition not only between providers but between purchasers as well.

Clive Smee: Most of our discussion assumes that competition is between institutions, an assumption that I think might be questioned. The problem with the concept of competition, even in areas where there appears superficially to be some choice, is not whether there is ease of entry to the market but whether there is any ease of *exit*. For any competition to have real meaning, we have to be prepared to see institutions—if that is the level of competition—go. Most of the regulation, as far as I can see, has been about either avoiding competition or at least slowing the pace of change.

The chief element of regulation in the first year after the NHS reforms was the maintenance of the 'steady state'. Effectively, this poorly defined regulation added to the overt costs of change, but achieved few benefits, because benefit can come only from changing and moving things around, so it was a year which, by any definition, was disastrous in terms of a balancing act of benefit against cost. There still seems great reluctance to see any speed of change. This is understandable, not least because the public in general seem to be against speedy change. I note what was said about not moving a contract but relying on a threat to move it in order to change the behaviour of providers—but it has to be a real threat.

Being realistic, though, what is to be done about a district general hospital, much loved by the local population, that provides 90% of the local district service? The threat in these circumstances is at the margin, at the most.

Tom Treasure: I share the view that clinicians should be involved more fully in decisions about both purchasing and the provision of care. For all sorts of reasons, doctors have let the opportunity of involving themselves in important decisions slip from them, which is not to their credit.

I am impressed by the sheer volume of knowledge required by purchasers to make sensible choices. They have to handle everything from preventive medicine, through community care, to high technology interventions. Clinicians have difficulty in measuring good outcome for any of their interventions; purchasers have to do it for *all* of them and, in addition, make economic decisions. They have an enormous task.

In my specialty of cardiac surgery, decisions about purchasing may be relatively easy: for example, coronary artery bypass grafts are carried out in high volume in a uniform way. A more difficult area is thoracic practice, which is heterogeneous. Purchasers and providers in my locality both had key clinicians involved in the tough negotiations about this, and this proved helpful. The competing provider offered prices which we were able to show were totally unrealistic. Variation in cost is more likely to happen in heterogeneous services than for elective surgery such as hip replacement and cataract surgery which are much easier to cost. I have every respect for the desire of purchasers to build a knowledge base.

Tera Younger: We need perhaps to speak of the market involving creative tensions between active purchasers and responsive providers that will provide incentives to make changes in patterns of provision. There is a great deal of emphasis on the need for change, even if this can be done only at the margin.

Purchasers clearly have the responsibility to decide the mix of services the local population needs, as Alasdair Liddell writes on p. 28: 'The role of a purchasing authority is to identify the health needs of its population, and to secure services to meet those needs.'
The district health authority purchaser, working with other partners, needs to develop a process for setting priorities. All district health authorities are now required to produce five-year health strategies, to develop some long-term priorities, and to use these as a basis for developing an annual purchasing plan. There has been too much short-termism, and there needs to be this longer

priority-setting process. As to clinicians, our most effective purchaser has worked closely with its principal provider, negotiating with clinicians and managers of the clinical units, and negotiating protocols of care. In some cases, provider unit managers have asked the purchaser whether he could provide some leverage to help them manage their clinicians more effectively. This is a potential role that can come from the process of negotiation.

Comparative information is also needed about care and outcomes, so that purchasers and providers can compare performance and help induce whatever kind of leverage there is for change in the market system.

In terms of the role of the intermediate tier in sorting out relationships, I think the Department of Health can play a role here, helping to provide an information base that would provide comparative information on an institution and district basis. This could open up dialogue with clinicians about differences in the ways in which care is provided.

Richard Thomson: Further clarity is needed about what is meant by regulation of the market. To take a cricketing analogy, if the England Test team repeatedly lost by being bowled out for less than 100 runs, one way to resolve that would be for the Test and County Cricket Board to change the regulations. For example, slip fielders might be required to stand 30 yards behind the bat, bats be made wider so that the bowler would find it harder to hit the wicket, or catches be taken with one hand rather than two—these changes to apply only to England! But that, I suggest, would be an inappropriate way of creating change in the pattern of results. Any improvement should rather be based on better developing the skills and abilities of the present county cricketers, and also on increasing investment into up-and-coming cricketers, with a view to creating better performances over time.

If regulation is seen purely as a sort of reactive response to media problems, as illustrated in the cricketing example, it could become destabilising, particularly if it is unpredictable or interfering. However, some longer-term strategy needs to be built into the regulatory role, whether at the intermediate tier or national level, particularly if we are to help the market to deliver the aims of *The Health of the Nation.*[1]

Anthony Hopkins: This last point is, I believe, important. Regulation has to be smooth and long-term, rather than a sort of jittery response to short-term variations. Sir William Doughty's contribution on p. 49 was also helpful—that perhaps we should start by thinking what *cannot* be managed by the market. We do not want to try to regulate everything—that would be very much against the spirit of the reforms.

Several people have underlined the need for information. It is necessary to know what is going on before we can begin to regulate, but it does not help us decide *how* to regulate.

Tera Younger and others have mentioned the need to set priorities, because presumably we have to regulate towards those priorities. Our thoughts about regulation cannot be entirely separated from thoughts about priorities and rationing.

Alan Langlands: We must remember the context of our discussion. Superimposed upon a consideration of how to handle the next stage of the NHS reforms are some other powerful items of legislation and government intervention, including *The Health of the Nation* strategy,[1] *Caring for People,*[2] *The Patient's Charter,*[3] and the revised general practitioner contract. All these endeavours add up to a coherent and internally consistent policy. We will not be dealing with matters in isolation over the next couple of years, but with the effects of all this legislation. We need look no further than London to recognise that the combined effects of the internal market, community care legislation and the Tomlinson report[4] are already beginning to interact in ways that are difficult to predict.

Clive Smee made three principal points: first, about structural changes (to which I would add systems changes) which have preoccupied us in the last couple of years and which he suggests are likely to settle down. I think he is right, but it should not be taken to mean that there is no further work to be done in these areas. Aspects of information management and the development of pricing and costing have already been mentioned. The building blocks for the contracting system, even at a rudimentary level, are not yet fully in place.

Secondly, he discussed (p. 8) the behavioural adjustments that need to work through the system in the wider sense of suggesting (as does Ian Carruthers on p. 40) that we have taken a conservative approach in the early stages of these changes, but that there has been no real threat to the financial viability of institutions. We have therefore moved into a second financial year in which more than £100 million is being spent propping up London teaching hospitals while we think about how best they might be changed.

I agree with his third point that many of the controls and disciplines of the old command system are still in place. Although colleagues have described one or two examples of progressive purchasing, examples of progressive *market management* have not been given.

I reinforce Tom Treasure's point that skill and sophistication are needed to handle the purchasing job that has been given to district health authorities. There is a lot of discussion at the moment about 'knowledge-based purchasing', but how many organisations are anywhere near that? The current managerial capacity of both purchasers and providers to handle major change has also to be questioned.

Against this background there is the huge task of moving from the previous steady state to a smooth take-off of a reorganised health service, and then to some sort of cruising speed. Some time could usefully be spent thinking about how to achieve this.

David Johnson argues (p. 48) that, as we go into the third year of the NHS reforms, we ought to look critically at what we are getting out of them. Others may feel that it is early days, and that it would be right to let some of these changes work through before a fuller evaluation is made. I am on the side of having a critical look soon, not because I think it is sensible to expect much at this stage, but because we are entering a year of tight public spending in which the NHS reforms, whether or not we either like it or are ready, will be fairly thoroughly road-tested. If we are to survive such a test, a good deal more clarity is needed about how the health service is to be run through the internal market.

We need to spell out some of the differences between management and regulation, to think about where regulatory functions are currently performed and whether that is appropriate for the future, to do more than use slogans like 'light touch' or 'oversight', and to find some examples that will help us understand what they mean in practice.

Brendan Devlin: In March 1993, hospitals in the Northern Region faced chaos due to funds running out at the end of the financial year, purchasers threatening to change contracts and then not changing them—and so on. As a surgeon, I like to know whether or not I shall be operating next week so that I can inform the patients. The discussion at this workshop is interesting—but perhaps 'theological' and not relevant to me as a clinician, although I am interested in the overall philosophy behind it. I would like to be able to tell my constituents that some progress has been made, and what that progress is. Progress is an iterative process: we need to know where we want to get, how we are going to get there, and to have some measurement instrument to assess where we are.

Anthony Hopkins: Alan Langlands and Brendan Devlin have both made the rather similar point that somehow we have to make operational these rather 'theological' ideas. It is all very well speaking about 'light touches', but it has to be stated what is a light touch, who is to touch and whom is to be touched. We need to be more concrete in our discussions.

Bruce Campbell: Market regulation is only one of a huge number of changes currently affecting clinicians and with which they have difficulty in coping. I would like to have some vision, as would my colleagues, about this smooth take-off into some other realm as to whether this is a period of change that will propel us into a rather smoother state, or into a period of constant uncertainty. One of the principal worries of clinicians is that at the end of this period of change we will enter another period of constant change in which competition will have 'bitty' changes all the time, so that it will be impossible to plan our services for the next year or the next five years. Or are we saying that the current changes are a major disruption which has to be put up with in order to get into a rather better steady state?

Anthony Hopkins: A plea for a period of organisational stability in which clinicians can work their best has been raised at a number of other recent meetings.

Alan Langlands: I think it is naive to think that we will somehow come up with an elegant organisational means of operating the internal market in health care, that will then achieve a state of equilibrium. The factors driving change in health care, not just in this country but worldwide, are wider issues of demography, technological advance, the world economy and increasing consumerism.

I would hope that all those who work in the NHS might achieve a situation in which they operate in an environment that feels more free from hassles than the current environment; in other words, that some of the basic organisational and systems issues have been sorted out, that 'noise' and these practical difficulties have been dealt with, so that we might together tackle the much wider set of problems thrown up by the social and economic environment in which everyone is having to operate.

The idea that the provision of health care in this country over the next ten years will be smooth and straightforward is one which I have tremendous difficulty in accepting, as do, I believe, governments and most people in the civilised world. Hillary Rodham Clinton's commission on health reform in the USA is struggling with some of these big issues even more than we are. I would like to make our system of health care more free of hassle, but we should not think that there is some ideal state towards which the internal market will move us.

Sir William Doughty: I would be interested in views about the introduction of clinical directorates, where ideally (though this is not so everywhere) the clinical director holds a budget, and hopefully has a good business manager. It seems to me a useful move that will bring doctors back into the mainstream of management decisions, an omission noted by Tom Treasure on p. 51.

Brendan Devlin: I think clinical directors are useful, and should bring doctors back into the mainstream of management. The problem is that to have a good clinical director you have to get a good clinician, and good clinicians are hardworking and busy people. They need support from good business managers if they are to be successful—which I fear is the weak link here. Chief executives do not, by and large, like having good business managers floating round hospitals: if they are good, they are incorporated into central management; if free-ranging, they represent competition in the management structure. I would like to see some clinical directors as non-executive directors of trust boards in different areas, advising management on other sites.

John Grimley Evans: I also am enthusiastic about clinical directorates, but there are two problems with them. First, when a clinical director gets appointed for 'life', he or she often finishes up being a member of 'them'—the management—rather than 'one of us'—the clinicians. A rotating clinical directorship within departments is excellent because it brings everybody's personal commitment to the system over time. I would also emphasise the need to have adequate administrative support. One problem, of course, is that there is internal competition within provider units, which means that the business manager, who supports the directorate, may be fighting against the overall strategy of the unit.

David Johnson: It is essential to ensure that clinical directors have adequate support from middle managers. We have provided this and have derived some benefits from it. This is not to say that the arrangement works perfectly, but I believe that the clinical directors at my hospital are appropriately engaged in making decisions about running the hospital. I am not trying to turn them into managers but to engage them for a small amount of their time, continuing to try to ensure the balance between their clinical practice and management responsibilities.

I agree that the best clinical directors are often the best clinicians, in terms of being the busiest clinicians, and finding time to carry out the role is often difficult. On p. 98, I outline how clarity of purpose and direction is a necessary condition for the effective, efficient and sensitive delivery of health services. Clarity of the role of clinical director is important.

The contribution of clinical directors at provider level can be made in three ways: first, an essential part of being able to manage activity within an agreed contract throughout the following year is to have clinical directors involved in negotiating contracts. They need not be involved in many of the lengthy discussions that inevitably take place just to make the process work, but where there are real difficulties, where there is need to understand different perspectives and find a way forward, clinicians have to be brought into that dialogue.

Secondly, clinical directors can make a contribution in setting the rules by which a provider organisation works. They play this role in my organisation in terms of operational management: they set the rules and then persuade their colleagues to work within them. This is effectively the function of the hospital management group on which they sit and which I chair.

Thirdly, they have an essential role in setting the future direction of services and of the organisation as a whole.

Anthony Hopkins: The Royal College of Physicians, with the King's Fund, has recently published a small book on clinical directorates.[5] The issues raised by Grimley Evans and Brendan Devlin were prominent in our discussions before publication, that effective clinical directors are usually busy clinicians, and diversion from clinical work may lead to loss of credibility. Business managers may see their primary loyalty either to the directorate or to central management; the nurse manager may see hers to the directorate or to the central nursing hierarchy. A surprising number of clinical directors report that they have had no input to the contracts for the services which they are contracted to deliver.

Malcolm Clarke: As a manager who has come from outside the health service, I sometimes find mystifying the degree of problems which people seem to have about these interprofessional relationships in a hospital setting. Other parts of the public sector seem able to operate a corporate management structure with people from different disciplines and professional backgrounds without these kinds of problems. I am not sure why this should be, and can only assume that health professional loyalties are deeply rooted.

There has been some frustration that political pressures are stopping hospitals closing and in other ways interfering with the smooth running of the market. We are deceiving ourselves if we think that we will ever operate without that kind of political regulation, and we have to accept it will always be present because the NHS has a high political profile. Political influence also means that

there will always be contradictions: for example, five-year purchasing plans will not be the reality for many purchasers, but rather whether activity has continued to increase at the defined rate and waiting lists continued to drop. If not, assuming political interests are the same, action on the waiting list will override any long-term plan, however carefully structured.

Rudolf Klein: I want to consider further exactly what we mean by 'regulation', a term we have used so far in many different senses. I suggest the following framework for its consideration: we are talking about structures of:

- markets;
- processes;
- products.

First, I am not sure whether we ought to talk about the *regulation of market structure*, which I suspect is a management function. In market structure we are concerned with the policies that affect ease of entry to and of exit from markets. If we are interested in competition, we have to consider how competition can coexist with restrictive manpower policies, a point not discussed so far.

Secondly, there is *regulation of processes*, which I think is the right use of the word 'regulation'. For example, we have not talked much about what rules should be set for the contracting process. Should more time be spent on setting rules of accountancy for the way in which prices are set? It has been stated that many providers set prices although they do not know how to do it. This seems to me where regulation has a real function.

Thirdly, *regulation of products* is how 'regulation' is usually used in other policy areas, in talking about consumer protection and about setting standards for the quality of goods that can be sold. (Incidentally, I agree that information is crucial, but it does not necessarily have to be generated from the centre. Why not award contracts to those providers who can produce decent information? This seems to me worth pursuing.)

These are three different categories of regulation, all of which imply the involvement of different sets of actors at different levels—hence the argument about what the health regions or other intermediate bodies should do. I do not think that the same answers will necessarily always be given—it depends on which of the three categories is examined.

To return to manpower, I would use the old-fashioned word 'planning' (not a popular word these days). Regulation, in an odd sort of way, seems to be the acceptable face of planning. Manpower planning is probably key to this, but manpower cannot be planned at purchaser or regional level: it is a national function.

Finally, on Alan Langlands' metaphor of a smooth take-off (p. 54), how will we know when the cruising speed has been reached? What are the policy objectives that the NHS Management Executive is trying to reach?

Alan Langlands: The policy objectives of the NHS Management Executive could be defined in many ways and trying to summarise them in a few words may sound glib. They could be summarised in terms of responsive purchasers, greater opportunities for patients and general practitioners to influence the way in which health care is delivered, and/or a provider market that works towards improvements in efficiency, effectiveness and outcomes. These objectives might be thought to be the reason for having an internal market in the first place.

Rudolf Klein: The word 'competition' is missing from those objectives. Is competition, as such, one of the indicators?

Alan Langlands: I think competition is a means to an end. Efficiency, effectiveness and improved outcomes may be achieved either by competition or through some other sort of organisational arrangement.

Peter Coe: I think we are missing something about the culture of the market. Regulation is not to establish a steady-state cruising at, say, 30,000 feet, but regulation that allows the freedom to travel at 30,000 feet or 15,000 feet or even to fly under a bridge. The culture of the market should allow both providers and purchasers locally to be involved in flexibility and risk. Purchasers must have clinicians and other health professionals working with them to allow them to establish the nature of that risk. Over the last two or three years, most purchasers seem to have lost all connection with clinicians other than general practitioners, and I suspect many of us are now starting to rebuild those relationships. There often is a core related to clinical activity that cannot change. For example, training posts in surgery must be approved by the Royal College of Surgeons; if an accident and emergency department is closed so that the post is no longer approved, it may not be possible to continue with some types of surgery. Purchasers can influence other decisions however: for example, there are ways in which wards can be run without nurses, and community services without professionals. If there is a dialogue locally between professionals and purchasers and providers about some of those risks and freedoms, it is possible to respond to the different demographies and geographies. Regulation must allow a wide range of flexibility in the way in which services are provided and purchased.

Alan Langlands: The title of this book contains the words 'the common good', which perhaps might be redefined as the 'public interest'. We should talk about 'stakeholder interests', recognising both that the public are at different times patients, consumers, taxpayers and citizens, and also that there are other stakeholder interests—professional groups, the education and research community, and the government—with the task of handling sensitively the exits of some providers. This has not been done well in the NHS in the past, and I am not sure it will be done any better in the future given the overall political environment.

Tom Treasure: Waiting lists should surely be history and no longer exist. They should be the final, absolute test of a proper market. At one stage, a waiting list was the difference between the provision of the service and the perceived need for it. There should be no waiting list for a procedure; if there is, it reflects a lack of confidence between the purchaser and the provider. If the purchaser decides he wants to buy a certain number of cases and puts the money there, he can find a provider who will provide that service. There should be a smooth flow from the decision to purchase a service through to its provision. A turnround time of a month may be thought reasonable because this is how long it takes a patient to reschedule his or her holiday, make arrangements for the children and a will.

Clive Smee: The internal market is an idea whose time has come, rightly or wrongly, in education, social services and also housing. Managed markets are not unique to the health service, and I would argue that most countries probably have a managed health care market. A price mechanism is not used in the health service, and most of us would not want one because it would lead to great inequities, so waiting lists or times are used to try to match a demand that greatly exceeds supply. Whether or not we hide them is a moot point, but it would be a gross misallocation of resources to have no waiting times when services are mostly free at the point of delivery.

Some of the uncertainties being discussed here are affecting not only the public sector in other countries, but all large employers. There are new views on how to manage large corporations, whether they be in the public or the private sector. It is all very well expecting everyone to be fast and flexible and willing to change their job at the drop of a hat, but what happened to loyalty? Loyalty by people to a service, and by a service to its employees are issues that are currently prominent in management literature worldwide

Regulation is not a new function in either the public or the private sector, and there is a large literature on which to draw. Many economists believe that it is most important first to get the structure of a market right, and that regulating processes and products of the market are to some extent second-best. If there is a competitive market structure, by and large, there is less need for regulation of either. This is certainly the experience of the regulators of public utilities such as electricity and television. In most cases, the regulators of the old public natural monopolies have found that they can work in the public interest, as perceived in those markets, only by changing the structure, particularly by breaking up the providers into more competitive units.

My starting point as an economist is that, if there is a competitive structure, there is less need for intervention on behaviours, at least to meet the public interest insofar as services should be provided as efficiently and responsibly as possible. Rather than saying that structure is outside regulation, I think regulation must start by looking at the structure that we have inherited, and examine whether or not it is competitive.

Many of the pricing rules that are already in place and have been used from day one of the NHS reforms were introduced because it was believed that there was not a competitive structure—and would not be for some time. If there were a competitive structure, I do not think rules would need to be laid down about how organisations cost their work. If organisations do it in silly ways that mean they do not cover their costs, they will rapidly find that out. We know that a large proportion of the private sector cannot set its prices in a way to cover its costs effectively. Those who do this for long go out of business, or learn how to do it properly. The danger arises where there are monopolists who can exploit their monopoly position for a long time: it is to control these that rules are established. Other regulators of the public interest, in utilities, for example, have normally had a precise definition of the public interests that they are supposed to be protecting, notably monopoly pricing. However, that is not the only concern of regulators in either the health field or utilities—there is also the question of regulation of quality.

I agree with Sir William Doughty (p. 49) that it would be helpful to try to define what public interests are unlikely to be properly met through the responsibilities of the purchaser. The list of values (p. 27)—equity, access, efficiency, appropriateness, effectiveness and responsiveness—should be seen largely as values for purchasers. To the extent that the purchasers can meet the public interests in those areas, this limits the role for some third party regulator. One way forward might be to take each item on the list and analyse it to determine the extent to which the purchaser cannot be expected to ensure its delivery.

John Sully: In September 1991, I attended a rather similar workshop at which certain themes for action were discussed: financial standards, truth in advertising, standard contract conditions and definitions, confidentiality for patients and flow of data. How are we to move forward from this workshop in ways that will make a practical difference?

Alan Langlands: Some of the themes of September 1991 look a bit jaded, although one or two have been reinforced. For example, Wessex and West Midlands regional health authorities might think that regulation around financial standards needs slightly more attention than it did even then.* Secondly, there have been follow-on discussions with the medical profession around issues of confidentiality. At the earlier meeting there was little provider involvement and certainly little or no clinical involvement. In today's workshop, we have broadened our horizons, and are not confined to a discussion about provider competition leading to greater efficiency. There is much greater energy and thought now going into questions of effectiveness and issues relating to outcomes, and much greater emphasis on the need to develop purchasing.

References

1. Department of Health. *The Health of the Nation—a strategy for health in England.* London: HMSO, 1992.
2. Department of Health. *Caring for people: community care in the next decade and beyond.* London: HMSO, 1989.
3. Department of Health. *The Patient's Charter.* London: HMSO, 1991.
4. Tomlinson B. *Report of the inquiry into London's health service, medical education and research.* London: HMSO, 1992.
5. Hopkins A, ed. *The role of hospital consultants in clinical directorates.* London: Royal College of Physicians and the King's Fund, 1993.

Editor's note. Both these regions have been involved in financial scandals, with criminal charges arising from contracts relating to information management and technology.

5 | Two professional perspectives on regulating the market in health care

1. Tom Treasure
Cardiac and Thoracic Surgeon, London

Clearly, a lot was wrong with the old system of allocation of budgets to hospitals on a historical basis, modified by the Resource Allocation Working Party. These budgets were often repeatedly overspent and created great frustration. From the perspective of the specialist or surgeon with a busy unit and an expanding practice, it appeared that the incentive was to *not* do clinical work. The throughput of cases was driven by the clinician in charge, the committed nephrologist, surgeon or other clinical leader, who felt that his efforts were slowed down by less committed groups within hospitals—but in the end the limit was the available budget. Whether this desire to strive to look after more and more patients is motivated by conscience, compassion, ambition or some other combination of motives, the perception is of an enormous workload: a lot of people 'out there' need help.

A great deal of good and considerable progress came out of this arrangement (to which I shall return later), but the problem was that it was unresponsive to, indeed oblivious of, the health needs of the community. As Mark Twain said: 'To a man with a hammer there are a lot of things that look like nails needing pounding'. There has been some evidence that the number of hysterectomies performed may correlate more closely with the number of gynaecologists in an area rather than with the number of women, and the numbers of coronary angiographies and angioplasties performed may correlate with the number of cardiologists. In both situations, the patient comes to a specialist who is in a position to make the decision and deliver an expensive intervention without reference to any other opinion. Before the National Health Service (NHS) reforms, clinical services grew according to the enthusiasm and energy of the professionals (the providers). They drew from the common health care purse according to their own perception of need. Thus, renal transplantation flourished in one hospital, bone marrow transplantation in another. In the pioneering days that was acceptable, but later imbalance persisted in striking ways so that the organisation of what should be everyday services, such as urology, cardiology, joint replacement and day-case general surgery, did not reflect local need.

Meanwhile, those doctors or surgeons with a dwindling number of referrals could disguise this and appear busy by keeping their patients in hospital for a long time, and by allowing days and weeks to slip by with investigations and observation. The only pressure to discharge a patient would be if someone else needed the bed. It was only the pressure that resulted from a reduction in available acute beds in the 1970s and 1980s that reduced the average duration of admissions.

The allocation of resources before the NHS reforms thus bore little resemblance to health needs. A striving, vigorous group of specialists would get more for their empire than more gentlemanly groups. Political clout counted for a lot. Doctors did what they wanted rather than what patients needed, and career pathways and prestige reflected this.

Thoughtful health professionals welcome the NHS reforms which allocate resources according to health need. Outside agencies—notably public health physicians—have the responsibility of assessing health needs. An increasing amount of information is available about the effectiveness and cost-effectiveness of different treatments. But money must follow patients, so that clinicians earn income for their provider units in proportion to the work they do.

How can we teach the next generation of doctors in the market-place?

It has long been accepted that a teaching hospital needs more staff than a non-teaching hospital because some health professionals in the former are involved in face-to-face teaching of medical and other students, and in the training of young doctors. Teaching how to do an operation takes longer than just doing it. Furthermore, two are paid to stand at the operating table—the master and the pupil. There is also research to be done, papers to be written, and meetings to attend.

There are two extreme views about teaching clinical medical students. Some hospital specialists treat all medical students as if they will practise with unlimited beds and investigational facilities. At the other extreme is the ragged-trousered philanthropist of a busy general practitioner who points scorn at the silly and inappropriate ways of the teaching hospital. Instead, he explains how a different type of knowledge will save his patients a test or a trip to the hospital.

In the middle ground, though, there is room for good sense. One fallacy that must be exposed is that 'clinical material' for teaching is something other than the sick as they come to us. The teaching hospital surgeon who bemoans the lack of a 'lump in the groin' for his teaching ward round, while the cardiothoracic surgeon's wards are full, forgets that the students should be taught on the disease extant. If people with hernias are being treated cost-effectively as day cases in district general hospitals, with minimum disruption to the patient and family, the student must go to the day ward and theatre and learn how the work should be done today. Medical students must be 'educated' so that they can work sensibly in the next century, rather than be 'trained' to imitate the ways of the last. Market forces in their widest sense should influence our practice and therefore our teaching. Nevertheless, the special allocation of money to teaching hospitals for teaching and research, (Service Increment for Teaching and Research—SIFTR), must be maintained. Teaching hospitals are likely to continue to have higher costs than district general hospitals because of the extra duties they perform.

If there seems to be a difference between the way a trust cares for patients and the way we would like to run a hospital in which to train our juniors, the reason must be sought. Does the trust work to a lower standard because its goals are getting through the work faster and more economically? Is it not possible that being quicker and more efficient is a good measure of the quality of the service? Could it be that the traditions of the teaching hospital have been wasteful not only of money but also of the time of patients and their feelings?

When I was appointed consultant cardiothoracic surgeon at the Middlesex Hospital, which prided itself on its quality and thoroughness, it was immediately clear that the patients would have to move through the limited number of beds faster if I was to operate on any cases at all. The single-handed surgeon whom I joined had a high bed occupancy. Patients were admitted up to five days prior to surgery and discharged a fortnight after operation, this being accepted as the proper way to take good care of patients undergoing major heart surgery. A system was soon instigated whereby patients came for a pre-admission day visit for necessary pre-operative assessment and investigations so that admission for surgery could be as late as the afternoon before the scheduled operation.

The length of post-operative stay was also reduced, so that the patients returned home, or to their local district general hospital, after seven days or less, which soon more than halved the average length of hospital stay. It was surprising to find that the patients did not perceive this as half the quality of care, but actually better care, and the rate of post-operative complications was not higher as some had predicted, but lower.

There are still many examples of hospital practices being based on a perception of what is needed for teaching rather than what is best for patients.

Research and development

Research and development may be victims of economy. New methods take time to develop and the capital outlay may be considerable. There is serious anxiety that if patients and funding go to the lowest bidder, those who are researching to improve care may be starved out.

What is the evidence for such anxiety? It is early to say, but the expansion of video-assisted laparoscopic surgery and other forms of minimally invasive surgery in urology, orthopaedics and thoracic surgery suggest the reverse. The shorter time in hospital and reduced morbidity have encouraged these developments. Trusts will want to have these technologies on their list of 'products' available to purchasers.

Unfortunately, however, not all advances save money, and the reverse is often the case. Renal failure used to be an economical condition to treat. Modification to the patient's diet for a period, followed by death in coma, costs relatively little. Haemodialysis, chronic ambulatory peritoneal dialysis and transplantation have changed all that. Treating end-stage renal disease is now extremely expensive (albeit extremely effective) and there is implicit rationing. Will market regulation stop individual units doing pioneering work and centralise research into 'national flagship units'? Have such units served us well? Major clinical advances in orthopaedics have come from hospitals other than the Royal National Orthopaedic Hospital, in cardiac surgery from hospitals other than the Brompton, and in renal medicine from other than St Peter's, St Paul's and St Philip's Hospitals.

The professional in the contracting process

Consultants have reason to feel uneasy about the contracting process because it implicitly challenges our assumptions about their response to illness and the role of the NHS. For generations doctors have believed that they responded as best they could within their budget to the needs of the sick presenting to them. Outside the Royal Sea-Bathing Hospital in Margate is an inscription playing on the name of its eighteenth century founder, John (or Ioannes) Lettsom which reads:

> If any sick apply to me
> I physics, bleeds, and sweats 'em
> If after that they choose to die
> Why, verrily
> I Lettsom

Now we have to put in a price, explicitly in competition with others. The quality of the work done is open to the judgment of others: it may be compared with published standards, the performance of others within the same specialty, other approaches to treatment, or the outcome be valued in terms of the number of quality-adjusted life years (QALYs).[1]

Specific surgical procedures in the high technology specialties are perhaps the easiest to understand in this framework. There are substantial variations in rates of coronary bypass surgery in different health regions in the UK. In the early 1980s, the Thames regions had the highest operation rates in the country, rationalised by the belief that the apparent inequalities were largely due to patients imported from beyond the regional boundaries. Manchester has now joined the South-East Thames at the top of the table, South-West Thames lies in the middle ranks, with East Anglia and the West Country lagging behind. The provision varies from about 100 per million to over 600 per million of the population.[2] In America, a staggering 407,000 coronary operations were performed in 1991, or 1600 per million of the population. Good epidemiological knowledge about the prevalence of coronary artery disease in different parts of the country should inform purchasing, so that some fairness is created, rather than persisting with the inequalities inherited from the previous system, which was led by surgeons and not driven by the prevalence of disease.

Measuring outcome

Death remains the most important outcome measure in cardiac surgery. Although many cardiac surgeons achieve 1–2% peri-operative mortality for coronary surgery (St George's Hospital where I work is still just below 2% with our case-mix), the figures from the USA have gone up, and the UK 1991 register figures have also increased from those for 1990. The reason is that higher-risk patients and more elderly patients, those with less good left ventricular function, are now being operated upon. It is possible to correct for case-mix using, for example, the Parsonett scoring system.[3] Rates of wound infection, peri-operative stroke and lengths of hospital stay may be used as other outcome measures. Other specialties must produce good figures on the burden of disease, the cost-effectiveness of their procedures and outcome indices. This is not easy but it can be done. Without such information, sensible decisions are impossible.

Rationing

For coronary artery disease, as for joint replacement, cataract surgery and a range of other elective procedures performed predominantly for the relief of symptoms and disability, there is likely to be more rational allocation of resources ('rationing'), but that only means fair sharing of a limited commodity, so how else should we proceed?[4,5] It is possible to define the level of severity of either symptoms or risk factors that indicates early preventable mortality. If this threshold is not surpassed, perhaps treatment should be considered not yet to have been earned. Rationing is applicable to elective cases who can form an orderly queue. For other conditions, provision has to be made in different ways. Emergencies present and need to be managed as cost-effectively as possible. One example of this again relates to heart disease: about 40% of coronary artery disease cases present as acute myocardial infarction, without previous symptoms. Accidents are another example of conditions for which 'rationing' is not relevant.

Improving care as a social responsibility

Targeting of resources towards areas of relative underprovision is another way by which 'rationing' can influence the health of the nation. Examples include the elderly, and those with severe learning disabilities. *The Health of the Nation*, the first health strategy for England, also stresses the importance of promoting health and preventing disease.[6] However, there will always be a one-to-one relationship between a doctor and a patient with an individual illness. For the health of the nation, this may appear a puny and inconsequential confrontation, yet this is medicine: a sick person presents to a doctor for help, who does the best he can with the available resources.

Cardiology, cardiothoracic surgery and management

Many doctors are not particularly interested in the nuts and bolts of the organisation of services as they are being discussed today. Counting, costing and being accountable does not come naturally to them. Cardiac surgeons, however, are used to such exercises, as are obstetricians and various other groups, for example, pathology laboratories. For others, such as general physicians handling a general medical acute take, the issues of purchaser–provider must seem less relevant.

Nevertheless, for the reasons I stated above, if clinicians are not involved, either because they are not invited or because they choose to stand back, the task becomes difficult and the health service loses that core knowledge of what is truly important for patients. Clinicians sometimes stand back because they are intimidated to some extent by management, and are frightened of the power of the purchasers. If a bright young lady from the South-East London Health Authority states that she has it in her power to close down either St Thomas's, Guy's or King's just by shifting the whole of cardiac surgery from one hospital to another, we believe her. Such statements are inappropriately powerful and disruptive of clinical services.

Doctors other than public health physicians are trained to respond to the specific illness of their patient. It is certainly the business of medicine to look at health promotion and the prevention of disease, but the practising clinician may not be very good at this. Those who take the broader political or sociological view should recognise that consideration of the cholesterol levels of the population and the prevalence of smoking are very different from doing a coronary operation. People who do the latter may have little enthusiasm or grasp of why there is so much interest in the former.

Some clinicians also find difficult and potentially threatening the fact that some patients have conditions which are not economical to treat, either because they are chronic and go on for a long time, or because they are expensive in terms of the management required. Such clinicians also worry about the implications of the philosophy of the measurement of the quality of life, for example, by QALYs.[1] Assessed in terms of QALYs, hips are a bargain, whereas bone marrow transplantation and multi-organ transplantation are so expensive that they cannot even be countenanced. These issues will have to be argued: individual clinicians may feel under threat because such high technology medicine is their life's work, but they may also feel they have a mission to fight for the group of patients who unfortunately happen to have an expensive illness.

I believe that clinicians have to be involved in health policy in some fundamental ways. The most practical way is to be part of the purchaser–provider negotiations, so that purchasers looking for a reasonable buy for their money are properly informed about the issues of different case-mix in different communities, with different costs, and also understand the implications of patients who live in flats without lifts, as opposed to those living in comfortable semi-detached suburban houses. Clinicians may also be able to explain why services may be relatively cheap or expensive. Medical information is also required for overall planning of services.

References

1. Hopkins A, ed. *Measures of the quality of life, and the uses to which such measures may be put.* London: RCP Publications, 1992.
2. *United Kingdom Cardiac Surgical Register 1991.* Society of Cardiothoracic Surgeons of Great Britain and Ireland.
3. Parsonnet V, Dean D, Bernstein AD. A method of uniform stratification of risk for evaluating the results of surgery in acquired adult heart disease. *Circulation* 1989; **701** (Suppl): 13–112.
4. Carroll G. Priority setting in purchasing. *British Journal of Hospital Medicine* 1993; **49**: 200–2.
5. Tunbridge WMG, ed. *Rationing of health care.* London: RCP Publications, 1993.
6. Department of Health. *The Health of the Nation—A Strategy for Health in England.* London: HMSO, 1992.

Further suggested reading

Golhaber SZ. Coronary disease: angioplasty or coronary bypass graft? *Lancet* 1993; **341**: 599–600.

Graboys TB, Biegelsen B, Lampert S, *et al.* Results of a second-opinion trial among patients recommended for coronary angiography. *Journal of the American Medical Association* 1992; **268**; 2537–40.

Randomised Intervention Treatment of Angina trial participants. Coronary angioplasty versus coronary artery bypass surgery; the Randomised Intervention Treatment of Angina (RITA) trial. *Lancet* 1993; **341**: 573–80.

Treasure T. Coronary investigation: US doubts about angiography. *Lancet* 1993; **341**: 154–5.

2. **John Grimley Evans**
Professor of Geriatric Medicine, Radcliffe Infirmary, Oxford

Although my main concern is with the clinical care of elderly people, as a general physician I also look after those of all ages who need emergency medical care.

One of the main problems in designing services for care of the elderly and in setting contracts for them is a lack of knowledge, which may be distinguished from lack of information. I do not know what constitutes an efficient rehabilitation service. I have ideas about the acute service, and could justify it from a research base, and the design of a long-stay service is largely set by cultural values. For the intermediate and important section of rehabilitation, though, there is so far an inadequate research base to determine what should be done. This should be a topic for NHS research and, later, development.

Clive Smee has stated that competition was a means to an end. I wonder whether that is truly how a competitive market in health care started. Many people suspect that the market is not an empirical device but an ideological imposition. All good Tories since the days of Keith Joseph believe in markets in the same way that all good Marxists believe in the dictatorship of the proletariat.

The USA experience has shown that the market as a model for providing health care is more likely to breed abuses than to realise potential virtues. Hence we have moved into this curious hybrid of the managed market. How much management can be put into a market before it becomes no more than a piece of vestigial political flannel? I am slightly concerned that we might be in a situation in which artificially engineered competition may prove to be at least as destructive as the absence of competition.

If the new reforms were to be examined as an empirical device, rather than as an ideological imposition, they are clearly like the curate's egg. I would identify the good parts as the producer–provider split, money following patients, and the concept of contracts between purchasers and providers with a range of providers. But at the centre of the whole market philosophy there is an aching void: the absence of the customer, or, more accurately, the substitution for the customer of a potentially rapacious middleman masquerading as a customer's representative; a middleman who has a vested interest in preventing patients receiving expensive care that they might need. I am of course referring to the fundholding general practitioners. General practitioners are not customers, they are middlemen.

One of the joys of working in the NHS has been that patients have felt that the doctor treating them has no vested financial interest in determining what he offers them. It does not matter to the doctor whether he gives one treatment or another; he is interested only in providing the best care. Patients will no longer believe that of fundholding general practitioners, and this will produce a considerable deterioration in the doctor–patient relationship. At the moment, there is no system built into the arrangements that can prevent their abuse, and the void is likely to be filled by litigation, as in the USA. Lawyers will soon realise that it would be a good idea for them to represent patients' interests in primary care as they are increasingly doing in secondary care. This would be an expensive and inefficient solution, and would essentially represent top-slicing more of the health budget into lawyers' pockets.

I do not think it was necessary to give funds to the general practitioners, and thereby the means of profiting by acting as filters. The benefits of general practitioners being contract-holders could have been obtained without this unfortunate possibility that they can profit directly from the arrangements.

The absence of the customer applies also to district health authorities. I consider them to be part of the purveyor machinery, not the customer machinery. Chairmen are appointed by the government and, although the chairman of the district health authority will undoubtedly earn his knighthood by making the system work, he is just as likely to earn his knighthood by making the system *appear* to work.

How should we try to bring the customers into the system? I am not enthused by the idea of handing their representation to community health councils or to patients' action groups who, in my experience, tend to recruit people with particular axes to grind and who often do not take a global view of the needs and aspirations of the constituency they represent. One possibility might be members elected to the purchasing authorities, but my experience in New Zealand suggests this is not a good idea, because provision of health services by an elected authority tends to get distorted by the political ambitions of the people who put themselves up for election. I support Chesterton's view that anyone who wishes or aspires to political or elective office should automatically be disqualified from holding such office!

One possible way forward is the following: information is needed about the health of communities in terms of Healthy Active Life Expectancy (the acronym, HALE, is very suitable), to measure which requires community surveys of the prevalence of disability and of specified diseases. It is then possible to identify both how well we are doing in terms of the final common pathway of output of primary and secondary care and social services, and also identify those diseases which are significantly contributing to any impairment of HALE in a local area.

If such machinery were in place, it could also be used for soliciting from representative samples of the community their views on the services provided and what they really want in the way of health gain. As far as elderly people are concerned, for cohort reasons these aspirations and hopes are rapidly changing; the people who are old today are quite different in their expectations from the people who were old ten years ago.

Finally, I would like to see the opportunities of the new system realised in terms of the details of the clauses in the new contracts about quality of care. I am concerned that the people who will suffer most under the new arrangements will be those not accustomed to standing up for themselves—not the middle-aged and the middle-classes, but the ill-educated, the people who perhaps do not speak English well, and the old. For example, contracts for coronary artery surgery could specify that if x per cent of the local population who could benefit from coronary surgery are over age y, surgery should be undertaken in proportion. Clinical audit could establish whether x per cent of those people undergoing coronary artery surgery are of age y.

DISCUSSION

Stephen Henry: John Grimley Evans cannot know his general practitioners well in suggesting that their vested interest in preventing patients receiving care is an in-built failure of the new market. The motivation of almost any general practitioner who became a fundholder was to have a chance at last to facilitate change, and to improve the service to his or her patients. Most of them saw the immediate opportunity of being able to influence local clinicians struggling like themselves with a hierarchical service.

In the early part of the first year of contracting, managers and clinicians would both separately approach us and tell us to talk to *them*. It did not take long to realise that neither clinicians nor managers can work alone in any system, be it primary or secondary care. I will sign no contract without the clinical director having read it.

Agreeing that the targets, activity and outcome performance are the best that can be achieved is very much in his or her remit.

Fundholding general practitioners do not work in isolation any more, but in groups. Whether they work in big groups like the Dorset Fundholders Group or in small locality groups, almost all of them work in a cohesive pattern with their district health authorities. It has not taken long to realise that the immediacy of the individual patient's benefit in the surgery has little to do with running a health service: the individual patient encounter is a tiny link in a big chain, and the big chain quickly gets beyond a single practice.

What has been difficult in terms of the rules and regulations that are in place has been the sense of frustration at the nature of change in the regulations in the middle of the year. Some regional health authorities have different interpretations of the regulations, which have had to be challenged at high level. We wish to break free from this potential straitjacket to work on behalf of our patients, and involve them in the discussions about the future of their medicine. The patient is calling the tune, and nobody is more aware of it than the fundholding general practitioner. In effect, we tell our hospital clinicians to tear up the working rules by which they have run their departments, we are sending them patients with money following them. They should talk to their managers about what that money can do for their department and how they really want to start to serve their patients in a different way.

In the same way that fundholding general practitioners are working on different principles than previously, we are asking our local hospital clinicians to do the same by trying to accommodate patients at different hours, with a different style of working, and in different clinics. Most are responding dramatically. The freedom from a hierarchical management structure has left them free to look at their own departments or directorates.

As an ordinary general practitioner, I am aware of the top end of the health service, its national strategy and financial principles. I wish to have a stake in these, but am neither equipped nor trained to write them, but most of us can have a good guess about the likely possibilities. All of us, accountants, health economists, senior clinicians or general practitioners, can only play his or her part. All these reforms are a joint venture in which we must know our own position. General practitioners can learn extremely fast about other people's problems from their hospital clinicians and managers, from district health authorities and public health physicians, whilst at the same time running their own business.

To me, regulation means rules, and management is how those rules are interpreted. Throughout the health service, particularly in middle management level, there are people who are frightened about their future, they are clinging on to the vestiges of the hierarchical command control structure, and putting the straitjacket on any innovation, both in hospitals and in general practice. A 'light touch' in management is needed on the clinical side of life.

Ian Carruthers: Some of the myths relating to fundholding general practitioners have to be dismantled. The first is that they and the district health authorities are somehow locked into competition. This is true only where there is a bad purchasing district health authority. Stephen Henry highlights moves towards a theme of greater collaboration.*

The second myth is that, from the perspective of a purchaser, contracting is really about cost. This is true only when the providers just recharge their overspend because they do not consider new ways of practice or if purchasers fail to take appropriate managerial action. Purchasers sometimes do not have very good medical advice, and they need to distinguish between medical opinion and medical advice. The issue for me as a purchaser is how to get informed medical advice about services. It is inappropriate just to assemble committees of people from different hospitals, all with a vested interest in making sure that the resource stays with or goes to them. We are now working more in terms of having reviews of services, so that managers and clinicians together look at the issues over a period of time. How purchasers get advice about the best practice also has to be considered. It is often based on current practice, rather than on the best practice as determined by research. Clinicians have not been keen to debate outcomes formally, but they have been able to say by whom they would let their family be treated—so they do have some information about outcomes and other aspects of quality of care.

David Johnson: We must consider how best to engage patients in decisions about local health care. I would also include community health councils, local representatives, local Members of Parliament, and special interest groups. Providers also should ask themselves questions about how effectively they deal with complaints.

If my experience is typical, *The Patient's Charter*[1] has increased

---

Editor's note: Anxieties about fundholding continue, notably in the way that patients of fundholding practitioners may spend much shorter times waiting for procedures than patients of non-fundholding practitioners. Here must be a priority for future regulation.

the number of complaints, and changed their nature. Complaints
are much more focused, and often directly related to elements of
this charter. They often trigger an opportunity to sort out some of
the operational problems within our organisation. We have to be
careful not to deal with them in a defensive way, that they are dealt
with at a senior level, and that there is a degree of independence
in doing so. If complaints are handled well, some of the real concerns that an admittedly small proportion of patients choose to
articulate in a formal way will be addressed.

When involving clinicians in management, we need to ensure
that they understand that business planning is more than aspirations about how much more resource a particular specialty or
directorate needs, and that there is as much, if not more, concentration on deriving more value for money out of what we already
have.

Richard Thomson: At the moment most purchasers are not seen by
their local communities as their champions. Local communities
perhaps will align themselves more with their local general practitioners and their local hospitals. However, purchasers do have
some critical roles to play in determining the capacity to benefit
their local populations by effective interventions, and in ensuring
access to such effective interventions. They also need to ensure
that providers have the systems in place to monitor and improve
the quality of their practice, in particular to reduce the application
of ineffective or inappropriate interventions. Tom Treasure's specialty, cardiothoracic surgery, is an illustrative example. There are
undoubtedly people in the community who would benefit from
cardiothoracic intervention who are not getting access to it. At the
same time, studies from Nottingham suggest that a sizeable number of people are receiving inappropriate interventions, by professionally defined standards. A mechanism of rejigging that balance
needs to be found.[2]

The provider role in all this, particularly the clinical role (in
which I include all health professionals), is to demonstrate to their
purchasers that they have effective systems of quality improvement
in place.

There is a lot of talk about outcomes, about which I am slightly
cynical in view of the difficulties in their measurement. If the processes that are linked with desirable outcomes are known, we need
to ensure that those processes are in place. If the links between
process and outcome are unknown, that is a matter for research.

Alan Maynard: John Grimley Evans said that little is known about
the effectiveness of rehabilitation. There are seven or eight ran-

domised controlled trials that have looked at costs and effects, none of which would stand much rigorous evaluation. This is not surprising because a similar situation is general throughout medicine. Most interventions are unproven, which does not mean they are ineffective. There needs to be integrated into regulation some form of body that addresses the question of setting standards, based on knowledge of effectiveness and measuring health outcomes. In the UK such a task might be the function of a health standards board, which could also advise on effective purchasing. Paul Ellwood and other health policists in the USA have recommended an outcomes management standards board, which would collect data according to uniform criteria, and work with overseas data centres, such as any the NHS might establish, on outcome evaluation.

The medical literature is beginning to inform us about how better outcomes can be achieved through larger volumes. One example is that concentrating treatment for patients with acquired immune deficiency syndrome (AIDS) in a few centres leads to improvements in morbidity and mortality. Such observations from the research community need to be sanctioned by some sort of health standards board so that the benefits of research can be integrated into the service.

Anthony Hopkins: There is certainly research evidence that the technical outcome of care of patients with AIDS is better in geographically concentrated units that look after a large volume of patients. On the other hand, if everybody is taken 50 miles away from their homes to have treatment for AIDS, this may deprive them of their family and social support at a time when it is most needed. A possible conflict between the biomedical or technical outcome of care and the patient's valuation of his care may need to be considered.

Alan Langlands: Alan Maynard's point about purchasing effective health care has indeed been well recognised and already acted upon. In the UK, the Department or the Management Executive has set up the Clinical Outcomes Group, Bulletins for Effective Health Care, the Clinical Standards Advisory Group, and the Cochrane Centre. There is also the NHS research and development initiative.

Graham Winyard: Alan Maynard has raised the question of the effectiveness of health care, which is a principal component of quality of care. Clinicians and provider managers alike find it difficult to enter into a meaningful dialogue with each other and with purchasers about quality standards and the sort of service they are meant to be providing. The Royal Colleges are producing guidance of various sorts aimed in the general direction of purchasers. Here again there is some dissatisfaction, because technical guidelines are often not what the purchasers want.

Anthony Hopkins: Many health professionals have anxieties about guidelines which, when they are prepared, sometimes contain a lot of opinion and not too much research evidence. This is particularly likely if guidelines are developed locally, as they may then reflect only current local practice. It is time-consuming to review evidence for effectiveness in a structured way. To take an example, a group of cardiologists could not agree on such a simple thing as which patients with angina should be referred from primary care to secondary care for investigation. They agreed that the reason for their disagreement was a lack of research evidence. In such cases we have to avoid making any guideline statement, pointing out that there is an area for future research. We try to be as robust as we can about this in the guidelines co-sponsored by my Research Unit.

The original thought behind guidelines, when insurers in the USA first became interested, was to try to reduce practice variations and avoid ineffective care, so that resources could be spared for more effective interventions. However, the fact must be faced that a lot of patients *want* ineffective care. For example, patients and their relatives want speech therapy for dysphasia after stroke. In our present culture, it is difficult to avoid arranging this, despite all the research studies showing speech therapy to have little, if any, effect on dysphasia. Indeed, one study showed that volunteers working under the supervision of a speech therapist were just as 'effective'.[3]

Brendan Devlin: The problem is that if we come up with a good guideline on something, purchasers expect that it will all happen tomorrow. Guidelines take a long time to come into action, particularly those that involve structural changes in provider units. It must also be remembered that guidelines usually reflect the professional perspective, and patients may have different values. For example, a procedure such as prostatectomy may be recommended if the guidelines are followed, but many patients prefer to put up with their symptoms.

Graham Winyard: Among the regulators in the health system at the moment are the Royal Colleges, particularly with their interventions on education and training. Such regulation is not always welcomed by providers. We have in our new system purchasers who are also interested in the quality of what is provided. There must be scope for a constructive partnership which would explore for each clinical service what it ought to look like, highlighting the extent to which it can be justified by scientific evidence. The partnership would agree meaningful quality standards that are affordable and practical and could be monitored through a clinical audit process more harnessed to the mainstream of the system than being (as audit often is) something of an appendage. By its operation, such a system would automatically generate and highlight questions to which the answers are not known in terms of what is effective, and from which would stem a large research and development programme.

Tera Younger: The Agency for Health Care Policy and Research in the USA is developing national practice guidelines on a series of different diseases. There is now a guidelines 'arms race' in the USA, with everyone developing guidelines, and newsletters to publicise what guidelines have been developed. The Agency has been trying to grapple with the fact that guidelines can be well developed, published in a journal or sent out to every doctor in the country, without as yet much evidence that physicians change their practice as a result. The advantage in the UK (as Graham Winyard said) is that once the guidelines have been developed they can be put into contract specifications. In the USA contracts do not have service specifications, but merely monetary contracts.

Anthony Hopkins: The experience in the USA of assembling league tables of comparative data has been that doctors rather like them, because they have not previously had any idea where they stand in comparison with their peers. Publishing comparative data could be useful if technical problems about case-mix can be resolved, and if the information can be given in a non-confrontational way.

Although the burden is clearly on the profession to develop guidelines of good practice, the Department of Health and the Health Education Authority have a responsibility to inform patients about ineffective care. We hardly ever hear about this. In my specialty of neurology, people with headaches often want brain scans. It may be difficult to refuse a patient who wants a scan because the clinical characteristics of headaches caused by tumours are not particularly different from those of ordinary headaches. In technical terms, the sensitivity of the history in detecting tumours is low. Doctors have a responsibility to provide effective care but the patients also have a responsibility not to demand ineffective care.

There is, however, a just criticism about guidelines. They have been too professionally based and are not yet linked into purchasing (as Graham Winyard remarks). They are good teaching tools for house officers, registrars and so on, but are not yet of much use to purchasers. My Research Unit proposes to try to maintain academic rigour in developing guidelines, but at the same time work with purchasers on how they can be incorporated into contracts, and to identify meaningful measures for monitoring *clinical* quality rather than operational measures of quality, such as waiting times and so on.

References

1. Department of Health. *The Patient's Charter.* London: HMSO, 1991.
2. Brooke RH, Koscoff JB, Park RE, *et al.* Diagnosis and treatment of coronary heart disease: comparison of doctors' attitudes in the USA and the UK. *Lancet* 1988; **i**: 750–3.
3. Banton R, Enderby P, Bainton D. Treatment of acquired aphasia: speech therapists and volunteers compared. *Journal of Neurology and Psychiatry* 1982; **48**: 957–61.

6 | Judging success in the market in health care

Anthony Hopkins
Director, Research Unit, Royal College of Physicians, London

I start this chapter by what may seem to be a diversion from my principal task, which is to consider how to judge success *in* the market, by considering the overall success *of* the market.

A perfectly regulated market for health care interventions should, in theory, produce the best possible health outcomes for the population as a whole. As an analogy, 'the regulators' could be envisaged as turning a number of little wheels, all of which are interrelated, on an electronic control panel in an attempt to maximise the output of electric current. It is presumably with the output of this sort of model that the Treasury is interested when it determines how much of the national product to devote to health and how much to other sectors of the public economy. Such a model presupposes some sort of consistent idea about what we mean by 'health'. Current definitions of health are, understandably, either so vague as to be unmeasurable, or so tightly defined that they reflect measurable functional status, which omits other important aspects of health-related quality of life. Traditionally, life expectancy at birth has been taken as an overall measure of the health of a nation, and empirical judgement would suggest that this is a valid measure for countries that are still developing. For 'fully developed countries', however, life expectancy at birth or, for example, from age 70 may reflect increasing years of life of poor quality. A measure of 'health expectancy' is needed, these words being in the title of a paper by Margaret Bone in 1992.[1] The principal question posed by her (and many others) is whether the gains in longevity have increased the number and percentage of very ill, frail people who require protracted and expensive medical care and whose well-being is severely compromised. Health expectancy or 'HALE' as described by Grimley Evans on p. 72 could be represented in practice by the more narrowly focused *years of disability-free life expectancy*, but the principle could be applied to life free from all or any diseases, or their functional consequences. There would, however, be enormous operational difficulties about measuring the latter. There are now reliable scales for measuring functional disability, so at least disability-free life expectancy is one potential measure of the health of a nation.

Two further points from Margaret Bone's paper are worth noting: the first fulfils intuitive experience that, although life expectancy is greater among women than men, disability-free life expectancy as a proportion of female life expectancy is considerably lower. Secondly, some of the most common disabling diseases, such as osteoarthritis and sensory impairments, are non-lethal, and research efforts should concentrate on delaying the onset of these diseases if we are not to have longer life with worsening health.

It has been said that the National Health Service (NHS) is concerned not only with health care delivery, but should be concerned with health itself. The contributions to health of other sectors of activity in the economy are well recognised: for example, the provision of adequate housing, the alteration of roads to reduce accident rates, and so on. There is therefore a broader aspect of co-ordination, if not exactly regulation, and that is inter-sectoral collaboration with the aim of improving health. In some of these 'healthy alliances' the NHS may prove to be a comparatively minor partner. Put another way, years of life free from disability may prove to be an acceptable overall measure of health, but it will not be an overall measure of the success of regulating the NHS internal market, because of the importance of other aspects of social and economic life upon health.

The decision about an appropriate indicator of successful market performance to deliver the best possible national health may distort the market. For example, the NHS Management Executive might accept a (hypothetical) recommendation from its current Working Party on Quality and Effectiveness that two indicators of NHS effectiveness should be used to convince the Treasury that we are doing well: reductions of perinatal mortality and in deaths from coronary artery disease under the age of 65. It seems probable that health authorities and purchasers would then divert large sums of money to these sectors of health care provision, at the risk of neglecting other important areas, simply on the grounds that by doing so, and by having a measurable impact in these areas, more funds would be obtained in successive years. Developing a small set of measures could thus create a perverse incentive to skew the distribution of resources towards those services covered by the measures.

Although I have focused the discussion so far on life expectancy free from disability, there are other potential ways of measuring a

population's 'health.' For example, repeated population surveys of
perceived health and functional status by Hugh Markowe's unit at
the Department of Health, successful market regulation, and
'healthy alliances' should in theory improve the health of random
samples of the population as the years go by. Another measure of
total population 'health' which is favoured by some is years of life
'lost' from certain disorders. For example, years of life 'lost' by pre-
mature coronary artery disease, accidents, and other *Health of the
Nation*[2] priorities could be aggregated, and this total would hopefully fall with interventions by the NHS and other sectors.

The concept of market regulation being required to maximise
the health gain of a population can be applied also to smaller units
of population in the territory of a health authority. The question
then becomes whether a health authority can regulate its providers
to maximise health gain for its population. As the title of this chapter indicates, health authorities and other purchasers need some
measure of their success in accomplishing this. If success is not
achieved, 'regulation' by some mechanism will be required.

The framework in which success of the market may be judged is
broadly as follows: the health needs of the local population must
first be identified, usually adding the rider that a 'need' is a need
only if there is an effective intervention that could make a difference to health status. This no doubt works well if there is a clearly
defined entity such as pain on walking which is relieved by a hip
replacement, but the concept is not adequate for addressing the
much broader health needs perceived by the population. For
example, there is a need for reassurance in relation to trouble-
some events such as chest and bowel pain not due to clearly identi-
fiable disease. Such needs are not clearly defined in any of the
needs assessment programmes now underway.

If the many unidentified needs are ignored for the moment,
consider the flow chart shown in Fig. 1. The better health status to
the right is an outcome attributable to the effective intervention
that has met the need. Regulation of local markets must therefore
consider not only identifying as many needs as possible, but also
ensure that effective interventions are available to meet them.
Judging success also requires that outcomes are captured in some
way in order to measure whether the needs have actually been met,
and health status improved. A successfully regulated market should
improve health status across the entire range of health needs.

The Department of Health and the NHS Management Executive, as well as many health service researchers, are working with
this simple model of health care. For example, the appraisal of

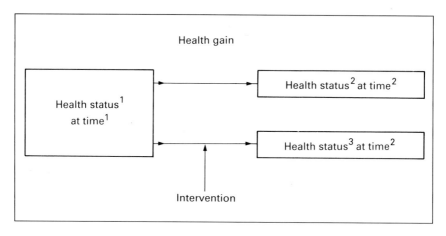

Fig. 1. *The health gain attributable to an intervention = (Health status³ at time²) minus (Health status² at time²)*

effectiveness is being undertaken by the Cochrane Centre at Oxford and the Effective Health Care Bulletins published by the School of Public Health in Leeds, in association with the Department of Health and the Research Unit of the Royal College of Physicians. The question of outcome measurement is being considered by Azim Lakhani's Outcomes Unit at the Department of Health. There is certainly no shortage of energy directed at developing this model, but there is of course one major weakness in the model insofar as it affects market regulation. Consider if, as a result of considerable research effort, it were possible to develop measures of outcome after a simple technical procedure such as a hip replacement (to continue with one of the examples listed above). Such a model would need to take into account both the natural history, including occasional spontaneous improvement, in those who did not have an operation, and also measures of case severity and co-morbidity that might influence outcome. If all these could be taken into account, it might be possible to regulate the market to maximise health outcome for this particular health need. A lot of money could be put into training hip surgeons, and into post-operative physiotherapy. As an extreme example, regulation could ensure that those units with poor outcomes on patients without significant co-morbidity could not continue operating until their surgeons had been on a course of further training. Alternatively, purchasers could manage the market informally by moving their contracts from such poor quality units.

However, the principal difficulty with this simple model is the enormous variety of health needs. So far missing in any consideration of market regulation is how to order the priorities of resource allocation to those various needs. For example, a trust might decide that little money was to be made in providing good services for elderly people, but that it could provide hip replacements with highly successful outcomes. The health authority would then need to step in and regulate the provision of services so that the needs of elderly people were met.

In summary, therefore, market regulation will have to include regulation of both the range and quality of services provided. The question of 'rationing' has been considered at a number of recent conferences and in several recent books and papers (eg Ref. 5, page 70), but it seems clear that it has not yet been resolved. We are, however, rather further on in considering how to regulate for quality, and the rest of this chapter looks at some of the difficulties that might arise in relation to this.

First, the measurement of outcomes: we have to consider whether we are looking at the outcomes of preventive care, of interventions either in population terms or undertaken in one provider unit compared to those in another. There has already been a fair amount of work in relation to population outcomes. For example, target B5 of *The Health of the Nation* document, *Specification of national indicators*, is 'to reduce the death rate for lung cancer by at least 30% in men aged under 75 by 2010'.[3] Another *Health of the Nation* document, *Public health common data set, 1992*, shows useful maps indicating geographical variations in such outcomes, lung cancer mortality being particularly high in the North Western Region.[4] Another example is mortality from motor vehicle traffic accidents, in which East Anglia scores higher than any other region. Such maps and charts should be useful to health authorities in their requirements by regulation for purchasers to pay particular attention to disorders in which the locality scores poorly. The second example is deliberately chosen to remind colleagues again of the potential contribution to health by other agencies. Other potential health service outcome indicators have been reviewed and tabulated by groups led by Mike Ruane and Azim Lakhani.

One sort of market management in population terms was introduced in 1976 by the Resource Allocation Working Party, when the Department of Health began to manage the market to some extent by weighting payments to regional health authorities in which measures of morbidity were particularly high. There has been a similar market management in general practice, with inducement and weighted capitation payments, the success of which may be judged by the location of well trained general practitioners in areas of social deprivation and high morbidity. Whether economists would consider these moves as 'regulation' or management is open to discussion.

The way in which 'regulators' might judge the success of individual providers—variation in which might inform them as to whether regulation is required—may be done in the context of Fig. 2, which illustrates various aspects of care that may require regulation or inform the need for regulation.[5,6,7] I have already touched upon regulation by the Resource Allocation Working Party, which affected both *capital structures* and the numbers of *health personnel.* Regulation of the latter might include local variations in salary. If, for example, there is a shortage of consultant paediatricians skilled in neonatal care (as there currently is), the market in these doctors could be managed by salary inducements.

Moving to the right of the diagram shown in Fig. 2, regulators will certainly wish to consider *access* to care. Judging success in this field is comparatively easy, which perhaps explains the concentration so far upon its measure in health service statistics. Two examples of access are waiting lists for inpatient surgery and timely access by ambulance to accident and emergency departments (ambulance isochrones figured prominently in the Tomlinson Report on health services in inner London).[8] As measures of access are so familiar, it is not necessary to say any more about them. Moving further to the right of the diagram, to the process of care, the first word in the box is *appropriateness* of care, a concept

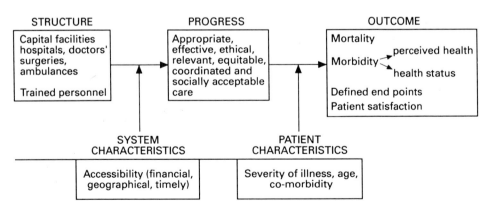

Fig. 2. *Schematic representation of some dimensions that it is necessary to consider when measuring the quality of care.*

which is exceedingly difficult to define, and even more difficult to measure.[9]

It must be remembered that patients do not necessarily choose the most effective treatment. They decide, hopefully after receiving full information about the effectiveness of all the different possible interventions, on the one most appropriate for their needs. For example, some patients may prefer to take tablets for angina rather than subject themselves to the anxieties and risks associated with major coronary bypass surgery. Others may prefer to put up with the need to get up to pass urine at night rather than submit to prostatectomy.

Success in providing appropriate care is most likely to be judged by one of the dimensions of outcome of care, patient satisfaction (to which I shall return). As to *effective* care, the Cochrane Centre and Leeds initiatives in appraising and defining effective interventions have already been mentioned, and regulators would surely be interested to know if contracts were being written for the provision of care of known ineffectiveness, such as speech therapy for language after stroke.[10] It follows therefore that 'regulators' will need to be provided with information both about the content of contracts and of providers' interventions by means of procedural codes. They will also wish to consider the *efficiency* of care, the extent to which resources are consumed by hopefully effective interventions.

How can the success of market regulation be judged in providing *ethical* care? This is perhaps the measure by which a health service might wish first to be judged, and the evidence is that regulators move in extremely quickly if evidence of unethical care is found, as happened, for example, with the 'kidneys for cash' problem at the London Bridge Hospital some years ago. Such flamboyant examples of unethical care are believed to be rare, but there are almost certainly far more frequent ethical failings: for example, when a doctor fails to inform a patient about all the various treatment options available, placing instead before the patient an option favoured by the doctor that reflects his or her values of the latter rather than what may be the values of the patient. It is difficult to see how such intimate exchanges could be measured on anything other than a random basis, but sensitive interviews with patients and doctors and subsequent ratings make measurement a hypothetical possibility. It is probably more important that regulators in the market continue to stress the importance of ethical care, and arrange a confidential reporting system so that all health professionals can channel concerns about the ethics of providers' work to professional bodies for advice and action.

The next word in the central box in Fig. 2 is that care should be *relevant*: that is, relevant to the needs of the community for which care is being purchased. An easy example to consider is a locality with a large population of black people. The family health service authority, district health authority and fundholding general practitioners would be neglectful of their responsibilities to such a community if they did not ensure that appropriate systems were in place for screening black people for sickle-cell trait, and for treating the many manifestations of sickle-cell disease.

The health needs of black and ethnic minority people can also be used to illustrate the next word in the central box in Fig. 2: that care should be *equitable*. Data about ethnic origin are now being routinely captured in health service statistics, although it is my belief that the complexities of assignation of ethnic origin have not yet been adequately recognised. None the less, regulators of the market should have ways of ensuring that black and ethnic minority people have equal access to health care.[11] For example, it has been shown in one district that those with names suggesting an ethnic minority origin spend longer on the waiting list for orthopaedic surgery than patients with similar disorders with names suggesting a British origin (K. Grant; personal communication). There is also evidence that the *technical quality* of care delivered to black and ethnic minority people is often less good, and that poorer outcomes cannot necessarily be ascribed to genetic predisposition to them. For example, the results of renal transplantation in black people are often inferior to those in white people. A recent careful analysis in one study, however, showed that black recipients received less well matched kidneys. If this and other factors were controlled for, the survival of black and white recipients was more or less the same.[12]

This takes us again to outcome—which is convenient because the last two items in the central box, that care should be *co-ordinated* and *socially acceptable*, reflect particularly on one defined outcome, the measure of patient satisfaction.[13] It is of course a truism that patients can be satisfied with very poor care, so the 'medical' outcomes of care should first be considered, and how the severity of disease, age and co-morbidity impact upon such outcomes.

As the title of this chapter indicates, regulators of the market must take into account success in the market when judging whether or not regulation of providers is required. The principal question is whether outcomes of clinical care can be routinely captured and controlled for case-mix severity so that comparisons between providers may be made, or whether there will have to be reliance on indirect measures such as patient satisfaction, choice, ease and equity of access, cost and volume of activity.

If the purpose of measuring outcomes of health care is to compare providers of health care, case-mix severity is of crucial importance. For example, a teaching hospital may well have worse outcomes after colonic surgery than a district general hospital simply because patients with more advanced disease are referred to teaching hospital surgeons.

As a further illustration of this point, the experience of the Health Care Financing Administration in the USA is salutary. In 1987, they published mortality rates for a number of common diagnosis-related groups for many different providers of health care.[14] Those institutions that ranked poorly obviously made the point just stated: that they cared for sicker patients. When corrections for age, sex and severity of illness were made, variations in mortality narrowed until virtually no provider of health care had mortality rates significantly in excess of those that would be expected by chance. The whole concept of *outcome indicators* therefore cannot be considered in isolation of *measurement of case-mix severity*. This point cannot be made too strongly.

It is important to recognise that there is invariably more than one outcome for any intervention, however simple. Even for a simple procedure such as a herniorrhaphy, the adverse outcomes of wound infection and unexpected peri-operative mortality could be considered, or the satisfaction of the patient with the advice he or she received with regard to return to work. In this example, with the exception of peri-operative mortality, such outcomes are not routinely recorded, even though they are all valid measures from the patient's perspective.

One useful way forward would be to develop a theoretical classification of outcomes. For purely illustrative purposes, without classification, Table 1 illustrates a number of examples, many that are important to patients, but not many easily capable of routine measurement.

There may be a conflict between the patient's perspective of what is a good outcome and the doctor's perspective. An example from the specialty of neurology is that, after a minor stroke, the patient's hand may (indeed often does) remain clumsy, which is a poor outcome for the patient, but his blood pressure may be brought down and he stops smoking, which are the best outcomes that the neurologist knows can be realistically achieved.

It is usually the outcome for the patient that concerns nurses and doctors, but it must be remembered that favourable outcomes for the patient may sometimes be unfavourable for a carer. For example,

Table 1. Illustrative outcomes.

Some outcomes that might indicate success:
  Years free from recurrence of tumour
  Years before CD4 cells fall below 500 per microlitre—a predictor of
    AIDS
  Successful technical procedure (eg 60% dilatation of a coronary artery
    stenosis at angioplasty)
  Relief of pain
  Relief of breathlessness
  Relief of diarrhoea
  Relief of depression
  Reduction in physical disability
  Reduction in handicap
  Reduction of blood sugar level in diabetes
  Avoidance of future problems (eg by immunisation)
  Patient's reported empathy with doctors and nurses
  Reassurance (how much, incidentally, can we afford to spend upon this
    most important outcome?)

Some adverse outcomes:
  Mortality
  Near death from cardiorespiratory arrest
  Deaths from potentially remediable conditions such as diabetic keto-
    acidosis
  Hospital acquired infection
  Blood transfusion reaction
  Prescription of drugs with known interactions
  Development of pressure sores
  Falls and other injuries to patients
  Complaints
  Litigation

Reproduced from Ref. 5.

a geriatric team may be pleased if they can get a frail elderly person
home, but this may have a severe impact upon the quality of life and
health of the carer.

Problems about the measurement of outcomes

With the exception of clearly defined events such as mortality, the
measurement of outcomes in routine practice is notoriously difficult. Even in randomised controlled trials of hypertensive drugs,
for example, considerable effort has to be made to collect such a
simple variable as blood pressure in a standardised way (should the
patient lie or sit, and for how long before measurement; what size
cuff should be used; what blood pressure should be taken as the

end-point; should the sphygmomanometer scale be concealed to eliminate recognised preferences for certain digits such as terminal fives and zeros, and so on?). In the following sections, some of the problems of measurement will be illustrated, using functional status as an outcome measure, improvement in functional status being considered a favourable outcome.

Choosing measures

A vast army of research workers is interested in the measurement of health status, and many of the published scales have suffered from 'tweaking' by subsequent workers. Researchers will argue as to which scale measures most meaningfully the dimension of health under discussion. My Research Unit, in association with the British Geriatrics Society, has recently reviewed the evidence in support of many published scales to assess the functional status of elderly people, and has identified a small number which it hopes that colleagues will use in preference to others, to allow some comparison over time, differences being used as a measure of outcome.[15] The scales may also be used to assess the appropriateness of placement for care of an elderly person. The chosen scales reflect physical function (Barthel), mental function (abbreviated mental test of Hodkinson), depression (Philadelphia depression scale), and so on. However, some colleagues spoke vociferously in support of other scales, and it may well be difficult to get everybody to use the same measures.

Technical issues of measurement

Whatever measure of health status is used, it must be *valid* (truly measure what it purports to measure), *reliable* (so that different people get the same result when they apply the measure to the same patient), *sensitive* to change (to reflect the effectiveness of interventions) and *without significant floor and ceiling effects* (beyond which the scale is totally insensitive). For example, the Barthel scale, whatever its other merits, is unfortunately relatively insensitive, so the score may not change even though an elderly person, his or her immediate family and the doctors and nurses concerned all 'feel' that the patient is better.

Ease of use

Measures of outcome must be quick and easy to use by people in the ranks of the NHS. For example, even if a scale fulfilled all the attributes above, it would be no use as a routine measure of health status for outcome measurement purposes if a consultant had to spend three hours administering it. It is recognition of this aspect that has led to the popularity of the Short Form 36 questionnaire used in the medical outcomes study in the USA, which can be completed by the patients themselves.[16]

Different dimensions of health

The Short Form 36 questionnaire is one of a number which attempt to cover the principal dimensions of health status. The best known example in the UK is the Nottingham Health Profile. Such multidimensional scales have been shown to be reasonably sensitive to patients' observations of their own health status, but their very multidimensionality raises another problem. How can a rise in score in one dimension (eg depression) be traded off against a falling score in another (eg physical mobility)?

The patient's view on outcomes

Patients themselves are best placed to integrate the changes in how they feel. For example, a patient at a follow-up visit may be more dizzy but have less headaches, but is able to say that he feels 'better' because he attaches more value in his feelings of health to freedom from headaches than dizziness. One aspect of outcome measurement worthy of further exploration, in my view, is work on patient-assessed outcomes. Dr Danny Ruta at the University of Aberdeen has shown how patients list a number of aspects of varicose veins that are important to them (aching in the legs, cosmetic appearance and so on).[17] A procedure considered to have a successful outcome is the one that has had most impact upon the patient's first-ranked symptoms. This seems an entirely reasonable perspective, but it means that comparison between provider teams of surgeons is made more difficult as the 'value-mix' of patients may differ.

As a further example, it is useful to think of outcomes in terms of reduction of a handicap, even though the physical disease remains the same. Disabled patients with multiple sclerosis who are reluctant to accept a wheelchair may discover that their mobility and quality of life are enormously increased once they do use one. Not only the technical issues of measurement of health status have therefore to be considered, but also the technical issue of the measurement of *values* placed upon those health statuses. Alan Williams' group at York is currently working in this difficult field.[16]

I have touched upon the patient's valuation of certain outcomes above others, and in general in this section have written about measured functional health status. Many colleagues and I are concerned about the research endeavours now underway in which valuations of what it is like to be in a particular health state are made by people with no experience of that state. In itself, this is an interesting intellectual exercise, but there is concern that such valuations may eventually be used to determine resource allocation.

Whilst writing about the overriding importance of the patient's perspective on the successful outcome of an intervention, it must be remembered that doctors play a role as gate-keeper not only to more technical levels of specialist care but also, in many instances, to support from social services. Again, citing my experience as a neurologist, many patients regard the outcome of a consultation as successful if they can take away a letter recommending to the local housing authority that they be granted a ground-floor flat, on account of disabling multiple sclerosis. Such an intervention certainly has an effect upon health status, however defined. However, at least in the initial stages of the development of our outcome measurements, our energies should be concentrated on outcomes more closely linked to a tighter definition of medical practice.

The next problem concerned with the measurement of outcomes is related to the *time* at which the measurement is made. Most discussions on outcome measurement implicitly assume that measurement will take place at the termination of hospital care. But, for example, after a hip replacement, the joint may not settle down and the patient receive the full benefit of his operation until after about three months. How are we to get systems in place for feeding data from primary care practice back into our information system, even if general practitioners and their nurses are trained in the necessary outcome measures? How will the quality of their measurements be audited? They will need to have some range of expertise in measurement across all specialist disciplines because of the undifferentiated nature of family practice work. Even for simple measures administered in hospital, research evidence demonstrates that response to a questionnaire can be greatly influenced by who gives it to the patient, and its timing in relation to some other event. For example, a patient's assessment of his own health status is likely to be much worse a few days after he has been told that he has cancer compared to a little time later when he has had a chance to integrate the knowledge about his illness into his outlook on life.

A final problem relating to the measurement of outcomes is the attribution of causality. It has often been said that patients get better in spite of, rather than because, of their medical treatment, and there is still some truth in this. If a therapeutic intervention plays only a relatively small part in achieving a successful outcome, the balance being due to the body's homoeostatic mechanisms, it would be wrong for the provider of health care to take too much responsibility for the successful outcome.

League tables

We are all aware of the current interest of government in league tables both in schools and in the medical profession. Each has a similar complaint. School teachers believe that social deprivation and different distributions of learning ability (case-mix if you like) are insufficiently acknowledged as a variable in achieving good examination results. In the health profession there are real anxieties that the complexities of measurement are not adequately recognised by those who are about to start constructing league tables. The message is that league tables cannot be constructed without having a sophisticated system of measurement. (See Refs. 5 and 6 on p. 16.)

Judging success—one way forward

I propose a work programme for consideration:

- A limited range of disease-specific outcomes for some common illnesses needs to be defined and chosen. It would be sensible to link these to the disorders that figure prominently in *The Health of the Nation.*[2]
- One or two of the many available generic measures of health status need to be defined and chosen, and their adoption encouraged.
- Parallel with this, specific measures of disease severity must be developed. Outcomes without knowledge of the process of care and disease severity are meaningless.
- Research needs to be commissioned into the feasibility of use of some of these measures in routine practice, not only in hospital care but also in primary care. There is a temptation to consider outcomes after defined events, such as childbirth or an operation, but the reality of everyday medical practice is that at least some of these pilot studies should be related to long-term care of disorders such as asthma, rheumatoid arthritis and mental illness.

- We need to begin to get experience with the analysis of large-scale databases. Much useful information has come from the Medicare data tapes (eg Ref. 18) and a lot could be learnt from the US experience in this field. This, and the research mentioned in the previous paragraph, requires a unique patient identifier, identification of relevant data items other than outcomes, such as severity of illness, co-morbidity, interventional procedures and so on, and, once again, *prioritisation and focus.* Not only outcomes of acute interventions and hospital admissions should be considered, but also the outcomes of screening and health promotional efforts.
- Finally, a common NHS written and, in the future, computer record needs to be determined for the easy recording of data items considered relevant in outcome measurement.

Conclusion

To judge the success of health care provision, outcome needs to be measured. This chapter illustrates some of the difficulties that will have to be overcome. Case-mix severity, the multiplicity of outcomes and patient preferences make routine capture of meaningful information nearly impossible without focus in a few key areas. The individuality of patients' problems means that measures chosen will almost certainly be indicators only for further enquiry. The state of the art of measurement of health service function and outcome is such that 'league tables',[17,18] which might lead to action by purchasers or 'regulators', are not yet likely to be informative in areas other than those of activity.

References

1. Bone M. International efforts to measure health expectancy. *Journal of Epidemiology and Community Health* 1992; **46**: 555–8.
2. Department of Health. *The Health of the Nation—a strategy for health in England.* London: HMSO, 1992.
3. Department of Health. *The Health of the Nation. Specification of national indicators.* London: Department of Health, 1992.
4. Department of Health. *Public health common data set, 1992, incorporating indicators from The Health of the Nation.* London: Department of Health and the Institute of Public Health, University of Surrey, 1992.
5. Hopkins, A. *Measuring the quality of medical care.* London: Royal College of Physicians Publications, 1990.
6. Donabedian A. Evaluating the quality of medical care. *Milbank Memorial Fund Quarterly* 1966; **44**(Suppl); 166–206.
7. Maxwell RJ. Quality assessment in health. *British Medical Journal* 1984; **288**: 1470–2.

8. Tomlinson B. *Report of the inquiry into London's health service, medical education and research.* London: HMSO, 1992.

9. Hopkins A. What do we mean by appropriate health care? Report of a working group for the Director of Research and Development of the NHS Management Executive. *Quality in Health Care* 1993.

10. David R, Enerby P, Bainton D. Treatment of acquired aphasia: speech therapists and volunteers compared. *Journal of Neurology, Neurosurgery and Psychiatry* 1982; **45**: 957–61.

11. Hopkins A, Bahl V, eds. *Access to health care for people from black and ethnic minorities.* London: RCP Publications, 1993.

12. Butkus DE, Meydrech EF, Raju SS. Racial differences in the survival of cadaveric renal allografts: overriding effects of HLA matching and socio-economic status. *New England Journal of Medicine* 1992; **327**: 840–5.

13. Fitzpatrick R, Hopkins A, eds. *The measurement of patients' satisfaction with their care.* London: RCP Publications, 1993.

14. Bowen OR, Roper WL. *Medicare Hospital Mortality Information, 1986.* Health Care Financing Administration US Department of Health and Human Services Washington DC, 1987. HCFA Publication 01-002.

15. Royal College of Physicians and British Geriatric Society. *Standardised assessment scales for elderly people.* London: Royal College of Physicians, 1992.

16. Ware JE, Sherbourne CD. The MOS 36-item short form health survey (SF-36). *Medical Care* 1992; **30**: 473–81.

17. Garratt AM, Macdonald LM, Ruta DA, *et al.* Towards measurement of outcome for patients with varicose veins. *Quality in Health Care* 1993; **2**: 5–10.

18. Hartz AJ, Krakauer H, Kuhn EM *et al.* Hospital characteristics and mortality rates. *New England Journal of Medicine* 1989; **321**: 1720–5.

7 | A provider perspective on the market in health care

David Johnson
Chief Executive, St James's University Hospital National Health Service Trust, Leeds

It is a fundamental principle of the reformed National Health Service (NHS) that separating the responsibilities of purchasing and providing care will lead to improved value for money and better quality of services through contractual agreements and a degree of market competition. The scope for instability and tension between the constituent organisations is much greater than in the earlier administered service. As the new arrangements are now working, questions are being raised about whether the internal market will undermine some of the fundamental principles of the NHS, particularly equity of access to services regardless of the ability to pay, and the clinical autonomy of doctors and other health professionals.

This chapter gives a provider perspective on some of the key issues being raised about the operation of the reformed NHS. These include:

- the legal and wider framework of regulations within which trusts now operate;
- the conditions for efficient, effective and sensitive delivery of health services;
- how providers can adjust to change with minimal disruption to services and staff.

Regulation of providers

The removal of Crown Immunity in the field of health and safety at work, including fire precautions, safety, and catering hygiene, has considerably sharpened the accountability of provider organisations in the new NHS in ensuring that the various legislative standards are met. UK and European employment and data protection legislation is also strengthening the accountability of NHS provider unit managers. The present regulatory framework is, however,

97

wider than these principal areas of legislation. In particular, the requirements of trusts as separate statutory authorities under the NHS Acts are clear. All trusts must meet certain financial statutory duties, and staff transferred to the employment of trusts are protected by Whitley Council conditions of employment. The rights and guarantees laid down in *The Patient's Charter* have for the first time set standards for patient services which are to be consistent across the NHS and for which providers are accountable.[1] The raised profile of health and safety at work is more of a priority within trusts than an integral part of the purchaser–provider dialogue.

The public accountability of trusts remains an area of concern. The statutory requirement to hold one public meeting each year is not felt sufficient to ensure that public accountability is taken seriously. Trusts are, however, adopting different ways of extending their accountability to the local public, including regular meetings with community health council representatives, with elected representatives (local councillors and Members of Parliament), and with voluntary and other agencies with an interest in health services.

Creating conditions for the efficient, effective and sensitive delivery of services

The creation of a loose federation of trusts within the NHS, in particular the freedom to manage services locally, has given rise to serious concerns about the overall accountability of the NHS as a publicly funded service. It is more important than ever, therefore, to demonstrate that managers and their organisations throughout the service are behaving responsibly and in the best interests of the patients they serve. A number of important conditions need to be created and maintained for the efficient, effective and sensitive delivery of services to patients. The first is a clarity of direction and purpose within all provider organisations, a clarity that must be shared between the trust board and key professionals. Large teaching hospital trusts, for example, can overcome the accusation that investment in expensive technology and specialist services will take place at the expense of local services by making it clear that preserving the function of a district general hospital within a teaching hospital is an essential part of their role.

Involving doctors and other health professionals in managing the organisation and setting its direction is another important condition. In some hospitals, doctors are taking on key managerial roles whilst maintaining their clinical commitments. This is possible only if they are given adequate professional managerial support.[2] Their commitment must be harnessed and not abused.

Partnership between organisations within the NHS, particularly between purchasers and providers, is an essential condition in making the new arrangements work. Dialogue between purchasers and providers has to involve high quality senior personnel and, where appropriate, professional input. For example, the negotiation of contracts without the involvement of the professionals who deliver services will inevitably lead to difficulties in working within the agreed contractual framework. The need to manage performance over the year and, where possible, the acknowledgement of pressures that may arise in the course of the year, have to be part of the initial contract negotiations. Too much attention seems to be given currently to rolling forward the cash limit rather than to discussing the quantity and quality of services that can be provided for the resource available.

Where providers are located near each other, the scope for competition is obviously greater. It is important, however, that this competition takes place in an environment that will not unnecessarily duplicate services to patients and therefore reduce overall value for money. For this reason, dialogue is essential between providers about areas of strength and weakness in the provision of services. Co-operation in developing strategic directions should also be achieved. As this happens, the fears about disruptive competitiveness within the NHS should begin to reduce.

In the first three years since the NHS reforms, there has been little evidence that choices are being made by purchasers on the basis of value for money. Purchasers must start making comparisons between the costs and quality of the services they receive from different providers: where similar services in terms of volume and quality are being provided for substantially different costs, purchasers should give notice to providers that they expect an explanation or a reduction in cost. This must begin to happen during the next financial year if resources available within the NHS are to be used more efficiently and effectively. It is certainly true that purchasers need better information about costs and quality, but this should not be an excuse for them to take no action to address the variations in performance which currently exist across the NHS and within individual purchasing boundaries.

The debate about differential access for fundholding general practitioners based on their ability to pay for services is leading to different positions being taken by providers, but there must be some clear principles to which all organisations within the NHS work. The principle of equity of access to health services regardless

of the ability to pay should be maintained wherever possible. However, the tensions and pressures created within the reformed NHS
that are leading to improved quality of services must not be
removed without giving these pressures an opportunity to develop
for the benefit of all.

Providers must get closer to the opinions of their patients and
other customers. It is only by listening to opinions and complaints
and taking appropriate management action to improve services
that the confidence of patients and the public generally will be
improved. The delivery of services will be seen to be sensitive to
patients' views when issues of importance to them are seen to be
taken seriously by professionals, managers and other staff in the
day-to-day provision of care. Users of health services and the local
community should participate in writing information for patients
and visitors.

Adjusting to change

Changes in the provision of services are inevitable, and the new
arrangements within the NHS have led to increased anxieties
about the instability of services and the implications for individuals. Whilst change is inevitable, it must be managed. There are a
number of ways in which adjusting to change may be accomplished
with reduced or minimal disruption to services and staff. One pre-
requisite, however, is that the general level of awareness and
understanding of the new means of funding health services must
be adequate within each provider organisation.

Communication is the key to this and must be taken as a responsibility of senior management. Adequate notice of change is fundamental in ensuring that change is managed. The contractual guidance currently in force recommends 12 months' notice of any
significant change in services as the minimum period that will allow
for adequate communication and for the proposed change to be
planned and implemented successfully. Adjusting to changes in the
provision of service will be easier when employment conditions are
flexible. Providers must introduce flexibility without threatening
the futures of individual members of staff. The annual review mechanism currently in existence for consultant job plans is one way of
ensuring that flexibility exists and changes in service accommodat-
ed. The ability of staff generally to work in different areas of the
provider organisation is also an important way of ensuring that
adjustments to change can be made more successfully.

One general theme of change in the NHS is the development of primary care services. Providers must be pro-active about this shift. Engaging general practitioners in dialogue with hospital clinicians about the future direction of services is essential to ensure that change is planned and adjustments in service provision made. There is not enough of this dialogue currently.

Conclusion

I have set out so far the framework of regulation within which trusts currently operate, some important conditions for the efficient, effective and sensitive delivery of services, and some ways in which adjusting to change can be achieved with reduced or minimal disruption to services and staff.

Much of what has been said in this chapter depends upon responsible behaviour by the constituent organisations and, in particular, their managers in the reformed NHS. There will, however, inevitably be examples where the regulations and conditions do not lead to optimum efficiency in the use of resources, and areas of conflict will arise. It is my view therefore that the internal market within the NHS should be regulated to secure appropriate service provision in terms of value for money, access, safety and quality of services, and consistency of operating principles. This regulation should be strategic in terms of service development and location. Arbitration may be needed as a last resort to resolve conflict between purchasers and providers.

The obvious location for market regulation is with the intermediate level of management. New developments there will have an important role in ensuring that new relationships develop effectively with constructive tensions, and in monitoring the financial and business planning performance of trusts. Regulation of the market is a strategic function that must embrace the different roles that now exist in the purchasing and delivery of health services.

References

1. Department of Health. *The Patient's Charter.* London: HMSO, 1991.
2. Hopkins A, ed. *The role of hospital consultants in clinical directorates.* London: RCP Publications, 1993.

DISCUSSION

David Johnson: There has been no consideration so far of the discussion that should be taking place between providers in some circumstances: for example, when there are two large trusts in one city, as in Leeds. Each trust has to be prepared to give up some things for the sensible use of public money and the sensible distribution of resources to provide the best quality of care. We have just started such a dialogue in Leeds, which should anticipate some of the changes that will inevitably happen and enable us to be more pro-active.

I have written about how both to adjust to change and to minimise disruption in doing so. An important foundation has to be an overall awareness in an organisation of the environment in which it is now working. We accept that the environment is now different, and that there are some rules of engagement within which we all need to work. This is an important part of the dialogue between managers and clinicians in terms of setting operationally the structure for the organisation.

In addition to the adequate notice of any significant shift of service delivery that I mentioned, flexible terms and conditions of employment (which have not really been discussed) are essential so that providers can get into a position in which changes can be made in a non-threatening way. The way to persuade a clinician that an alternative form of contract is a good idea is not to tell him that he will lose his job if the particular change has not been effected in two years' time, but to underline that we are working in a partnership.

Alan Langlands: I am sure that David Johnson is right to point out that providers on their own, or by talking to each other, might influence directly the future development of services. Purchasers and/or regulators are not the only shapers of the future. Some of the best thinking about change still happens at provider level.

Peter Shrigley: In September 1992, I and the chief executive of the neighbouring NHS trust, Rochdale, worked together with clinicians to combine ophthalmic services. The two trust boards agreed and on 1st April a seven-strong consultant specialty team became operational and is now contracting for work. Most of us believe that in the previous bureaucracy such an agreement would not have been achieved. Our success principally was due to having a proper brief, to trust between two neighbouring trusts, and a recognition that the service which has been created is a contractor now in its own right.

Clive Smee: Each year the Treasury drives us down an increasingly demanding path in terms of efficiency gains. I have been asked by colleagues in the Department of Health to help answer the question of how to know when further gains in efficiency are being achieved only at the cost of deterioration in quality of service.

Without a clear answer, we are disadvantaged in making a case for more expenditure for the NHS. Education, for example, has been able to demonstrate that educational standards in this country are towards the bottom of the pile compared with other countries. This therefore makes a good case for more money for education which, at the end of the day, means less money for other services such as health. We need to know how to judge in two or three years' time whether the NHS reforms have achieved improved services to the public with improved efficiency. Furthermore, if waiting lists are reduced, and consumer satisfaction greater, have these been achieved at the cost of clinical outcomes? How and when will we know? What small number of indicators can be developed to track this? The Management Executive Working Group on Quality and Effectiveness is beginning to grapple with these problems. Some topics will be handed over to the Director of Research and Development for further development.

Related to measures of quality and effectiveness, it seems to me legitimate for purchasers to ask how they can discriminate between poor and good providers. They can discriminate quite easily in terms of patient satisfaction, waiting lists and times, and a range of good management practices such as whether discharge letters come forward quickly, and so on, or in terms of time required for the patient to travel to the local hospital. These are the kind of measures now being used. However, I am still not clear how purchasers can judge on the basis of clinical outcomes, and in Chapter 6 Anthony Hopkins shows that this will not be easy.

If purchasers should be looking for quality and yet are not, how can that be known at the centre, and how can regions know without some indicators of the kind I have mentioned? Purchasers may be achieving tremendous improvements in efficiency, but at the cost of undesirable declines in quality. We are not yet asking or hoping for comprehensive answers, and know that the development of measures will take time. It would be helpful, however, to have a few indicators that we could begin to see as tracers, that could be monitored year on year, and which would flash warning lights when there was real cause for concern.

Richard Thomson: Some powerful possibilities for quality improvement in health care are beginning to be teased out by bringing together the components of national research and development programmes, the development of guidelines and protocols and clinical audit.

The possibilities for improvement may be illustrated by referring to an example from the Northern Region. Haematologists in the

region have a strong co-operative group that is continually reviewing the protocols of treatment for patients with haematological
malignancies, together with a system for implementing these protocols and auditing them across the region. The group also has a
system for collecting the necessary data to be able to evaluate the
outcomes as a result of applying the protocols. When questions
arising from such observational studies are raised, randomised trials can be undertaken to develop further their protocols.

Rather than purchasers making unilateral judgements about the
quality of the care that they are purchasing, there needs to be this
co-operative component between purchasers and providers, the
providers thereby demonstrating that they have systems in place to
show continual improvement in quality, and the purchasers having
systems in place to ensure the capacity to benefit their population
is being plugged into that purchaser–provider interaction.

Stuart Dickens: I agree that the notion that everything can be
achieved through the purchasing process is ill-founded. It needs to
be recognised that a good purchaser will emphasise collaboration
for change, which certainly means working closely with providers.
As an example, four purchasers and four providers in Birmingham
have agreed on the way in which emergency medicine and surgery
is dealt with across the city as a single contract. This has been
informed by the way in which providers feel they can manage the
work, as well as by purchasers' clearly articulated expectations.

I believe that a demonstrable audit trail is needed between the
key issues identified by our directors of public health (who ought
to be acting as a spur to health authorities on important local
health issues), the investment allocated to deal with particular
problems, and the outcome. If such a linked process cannot be
demonstrated, why do we exhort directors of public health to
produce annual reports?

John Sully: If I were asked how I would expect to be judged as a
purchaser, I would say that it would be by:

- fulfilling the annual corporate contract with the regional health
  authority;
- having a set of processes in place to do with how I work with general practitioners, both fundholders and non-fundholders;
- doing regular, consistent market research on the satisfaction of
  the population with its local health service and care. There are
  problems and faults with the measurement of patient satisfaction, but it is something that we take seriously;
- showing a measurable improvement in outcomes—I believe it is

necessary to stay in a place a long time to achieve results in health care;
- achieving these aims within a defined budget. We do not yet have a reasonable cost for the purchasing function, but I estimate that it should be possible to cover our purchasing costs within 1.5% of our total expenditure.

Stephen Henry: Purchasing cannot make a specialist a better doctor; it can only improve the service that he or she gives. However, purchasing faith, in collaboration with the local managers and clinicians, can restore a hospital which has been giving bad service.
Brendan Devlin: Comparative league tables can be further developed in surgery. We have done this for avoidable peri-operative deaths in surgery (the Confidential Enquiry into Peri-operative Deaths—the CEPOD Report[1]). However, we remain uncertain what to do about individual units or surgeons with many adverse outcomes.
Graham Winyard: The medical profession has to face up to the fact that the public does not have confidence that incompetent doctors are being dealt with. Until they do, they will press for things like league tables and will not be interested in the technicalities of case-mix and so on. They will ask purchasers and providers what they are doing about poor practice, and if nothing can be done, they will want league tables because that is the best they can think of for the moment. We need to start from the anxieties of the public, and not from our legitimate concerns about the technical interpretation of league tables.
Tom Treasure: I share the anxiety about what to do about poor clinical performance. It cannot necessarily be assumed that retraining is the answer. I could be coached for ever at tennis, and I would do my best and give an old lame man a half-decent game, but no better than that. If people are not able to do surgery, it is not a question of retraining: they have to do something else. Early identification of doctors who are not in the right slot is a matter for the profession.

Another tacit assumption is that there is a trade-off between thoroughness and quality, and that by reducing time in hospital, and by doing fewer things there, the quality is poorer. This argument is produced by people who like to use a lot of high-technology interventions. It is well-known from the example of day-case surgery that you can win both ways: there are better outcomes at less cost. More cost does not necessarily equal better quality.
Clive Smee: Ideally, we would like to have a system of measures of

quality and clinical effectiveness built up nationally from the lower levels of individual clinician and hospital. I do not know whether it is possible to move to a situation in which the information is kept confidential at the clinician or hospital level but can be aggregated up to show trends through time at the national or regional level. This would meet my agenda, but not of course other people's, including that of purchasers, who want to be able to discriminate. There must be some way round this or, at the end of the day, it does not seem fair to expect purchasers to be able to discriminate on quality. Purchasers can hardly be blamed if they place their contracts purely on the basis of cost, especially in the light of Tom Treasure's argument that low cost can also mean good quality. I am sure he is right up to a point, but there must come a stage at which costs are pressed down so much that quality is put at risk. This is what we are talking about: how do we know when that point has been reached? If we do not have some indicators of clinical quality and effectiveness, there must always be a worry in the public's mind, not just in the minds of health economists, that we may be reaching the stage at which quality is declining.

David Taylor: I am not sure that the pressure for league tables is really driven by consumers, as Graham Winyard suggests. However, the core business of the NHS is not only clinical treatment but also primary prevention, and, perhaps even more important, helping people to tolerate and live with ill health. Medicine is not just about health gain, but about dealing with the fear of ill health, the tolerance of illness, and with the reality of extended ill health. Indicators of quality are needed which pick up performance in these other contexts, not only technical measures of improved health status.

William Ross: I would like to remind you of the role of the Royal Colleges. The Colleges are charitable organisations with a Royal Charter and answerable to the Privy Council. Without exception, these Royal Charters require that the Colleges exist for the protection of the patient and the public, and certainly not for the protection of the individual Members and Fellows of the Colleges. One way in which the Colleges can demonstrate this activity is by maintaining the standard of consultants appointed across the health service. There is concern at present that some trusts are appointing senior doctors without following the statutory methods. All the Colleges are actively working on the development and evaluation of continuing medical education which may at some future time lead to re-certification or re-accreditation.

Conference brings together the Presidents of all the medical

Royal Colleges and their Faculties. It has nominees on the Clinical Standards Advisory Board, and is a constituent body of the Joint Consultants Committee. As the standards of clinical practice and the quality of care are at the heart of the activities of all Colleges, Conference is pleased to have co-sponsored the workshop, the proceedings of which form this book.

Reference

1. Campling EA, Devlin HB, Hoile RW, Lunn JN. *The Report of the National Confidential Enquiry into Perioperative Deaths 1991/2.* London: NCEPOD, Royal College of Surgeons, 1993.

8 | Regulation of the market in the new NHS: an overview

Carol Propper
Lecturer, School of Advanced Urban Studies, Bristol, and presently Senior Economic Advisor, Department of Health

Anthony Hopkins
Director, Research Unit, Royal College of Physicians

The chapters in this book reflect the views of individuals who operate in different parts of the NHS internal market. Some are involved in their daily activity in the provision and purchase of health care, others are in the 'headquarters' of the NHS. Despite differences in perspectives, a set of common themes emerge.

Several of the chapters list a set of activities that, in some way or other, are regulated by the centre, and it is apparent first that both those in the market and those responsible for managing the market feel that the scope and number of current regulations is large. Second, as the market has developed, there has been a lack of clarity as to what is management and what is regulation. The boundary between management and regulation is not well defined. One activity shades into another; one person's management is another's regulation. This confusion leaves participants in the market unclear as to what is mandatory and what is optional. Third, the regulatory function is at present performed by a number of actors. The Management Executive clearly has a regulatory role and the present regional health authorities have seen themselves as having a role. These roles are nowhere precisely defined. Purchasers certainly manage care by appropriate commissioning, but should they be seen as acting in some regulatory capacity on their providers, and where do these actions fit in with the actions of the 'headquarters of the NHS'? Professional bodies also have a central role to play in regulating the training and conduct of their members.

We should not be surprised by this lack of clarity. The internal market had been in operation for only two years when this workshop was held. The energies of those in the market have been turned towards understanding their new roles and the continued provision of health care. Now, however, the chapters in this book and the publication of *Managing the new NHS*[1] reflect a common desire to see this regulatory role put on a clearer footing. Most participants favour a 'light touch' style of regulation, but without yet being explicit as to what they mean by this.

Key issues

What is the aim of regulation?

Regulation is one of the tools to achieve maximisation of the health of the population by the efficient delivery of services through an internal market. Specific goals for regulation will include the protection of users or consumers, the protection of the taxpayer and the support of the internal market. As Clive Smee points out on p. 14, competition is a means to an end, not an end in itself. It cannot be the sole aim of the internal market.

One of the central tasks of the NHS Management Executive is to 'operationalise' regulation and to use it as one tool for achieving the NHS goals of effectiveness, efficiency and equity. Regulation is not costless. It may have perverse incentives. It should only be undertaken if there are clear benefits. Regulation is not a substitute for day-to-day management, nor should it be used as such. Likewise, regulation is not planning. An internal market may require as much planning as a centralised system, albeit of different forms and possibly involving different groups of actors. Regulation is not a substitute for decisions that have long-term consequences, such as the planning of medical manpower, or the location of specialised facilities. Regulation of particular activities may have similar effects to planning—for example, the expansion of expensive imaging facilities was regulated (belatedly) in the USA and this affected the pattern of provision. Similarly, self regulation by the professions to ensure adequate quality will affect the location and availability of specialist treatments. Regulation will interact with management and planning. Occasionally, regulation may be required when either is deficient.

Regulation should be pro-competitive. The regulation of the market structure should provide a framework within which there is regulation.

The regulatory framework should promote competitive market structures. It is generally argued that the establishment of a market structure in which there are a number of possible buyers and sellers will lead to competitive market behaviour. Regulation should allow entry and exit and aim to encourage, rather than to mimic or replace, the market. It is not always necessary to have many competing suppliers operating in one market to reap the benefits of competition. In some circumstances, the threat of entry of a new supplier may be sufficient to bring the benefits of actual competition. Such a market structure is termed a 'contestable' market. The regulatory structure should be designed to promote contestability in cases where actual competition is likely to be limited.

Within the framework of a set of regulations of structure which ensure that competition is promoted, providers and purchasers should be given as much freedom to act as possible, whilst ensuring that their actions remain consistent with the goals set for NHS purchasers and providers. In a sector of the economy in which funds are provided by the tax payer and treatment is allocated on the basis of need, not ability to pay, there will always be a need for targets which providers and purchasers are required to meet. Similarly, until outcomes of the interventions of health care are more easily measured, there will be a need to encourage effective processes of care. But the task of the regulatory authority should be to reduce the number of such regulations and targets to a minimum.

Regulation may itself create perverse incentives

The regulator will always have less access to information than the regulated, so cannot regulate everything. Regulation as part of the activity of the regulated bodies may create perverse incentives. The regulated will have little (and in the limit no) incentive to perform activities that are not subject to regulation. An example is the current efficiency index which rewards activity in inpatient care but takes no account of other clinical activity, so perhaps leading to an underemphasis on other ways of treating patients which other policies seek to encourage. The narrow set of targets facing purchasers is another example. Some purchasers have argued that the strong emphasis placed by the heaquarters of the NHS on the achievement of a narrow range of targets has prevented them from undertaking activities in areas they feel are important; there is no reward for carrying out activities that may reflect local wishes but are not part of the current set of targets set by the centre. This means, as one of us writes in Chapter 6, that regulatory targets need to be chosen with care.

There should be clear assignment of regulatory functions

The preceding chapters have shown that the difference between management and regulation is not always clear. Nor is it always clear who does what in terms of regulation. These roles must be clarified if regulation is to be helpful. A first step in this process has been the publication of *Managing the new NHS*. Figures 3 and 4 in Chapter 3 outline the functions carried out in the NHS and allocation of functions to the new structure. Paragraph 29 of *Managing the new NHS* records that 'The general principle underlying the allocation of functions will be to minimalise centralisation and maximise delegation of responsibility to local level while maintaining clear lines of accountability.' However, it is clear that the skeletons illustrated in Chapter 3 need fleshing out. Paragraph 30 reads '. . . working groups from the NHSME. RHAs and local purchasers and providers will consider each of the main functions in depth, identifying the individual activities and tasks which need to be undertaken and assigning them to different parts of the structure. From this analysis a detailed definition of roles, responsibilities, accountabilities and manpower requirements will be built up for each part of the structure.'

Interaction between the regulation of providers and the regulation of purchasers

Regulatory action on one side of the market will have implications for the behaviour of the other side. Allowing exit may increase purchaser power, at least in the short term. Allowing entry of more providers will alter the ability of purchasers to shop around and so may encourage more pro-active purchasers. Such interaction between purchasing and provision, coupled with the fact that regulation may have unintended and even perverse outcomes if not carefully designed, points to the need for a single authority responsible for market regulation.

This is recognised in *Managing the new NHS* by the integration of regional health authorities (formerly concerned with managing purchasers) and NHS Management Executive outposts (formerly concerned with the oversight of providers) into regional offices.

Professional concerns

The Conference of Medical Royal Colleges and their Faculties were co-sponsors, with the NHS Management Executive, of the workshop on which this book is based. It is right to conclude this chapter by recording some professional concerns about the market in health care, and about regulation.

Regulation of purchasing

Consultants may run through their contracts with health authority purchasers well before the end of the financial year, at a time when fundholding practitioners continue to have sufficient resources to ensure that their patients are seen promptly and treated. Consultants are particularly concerned about the resulting imbalance and inequity of access to care. This is an area of the NHS reforms that requires further consideration and development in order to set up a system that will require the minimum of future regulation. In particular, the lines of accountability of fundholders require clarification.

Training of future consultants

The reforms outlined in the recent report from the Chief Medical Officer's Working Group on Specialist Training[2] involve a merging of registrar and senior registrar grades as part of an overall strategy to reduce the duration of training whilst improving its effectiveness. This will require a change from the traditional apprenticeship-type training to more formal teaching, including the development of detailed curricular requirements for each specialty and objective attention of trainee performance and quality of training.

In order that training may take place in an effective manner and not be crowded out by clinical duties, it is essential that future contracting procedures include an educational component. Some regions are already introducing an educational contract, a procedure made easier by the fact that postgraduate deans now control fifty per cent of the budget for trainees. Postgraduate deans will be best placed to monitor the effectiveness of such contracts, although the Royal Colleges and their higher training committees will make their own assessment of the situation during their regular visits. Currently these bodies have an effective sanction in the removal of educational approval from junior posts. Under existing agreements with the Department of Health, trainees may not be recruited into unapproved posts. It will be essential to the future success of training programmes that this regulatory influence of the Department of Health continues to be exerted over trusts and other employing authorities.

The Royal Colleges have similar concerns about general professional training at the level of senior house officer. For example, the Royal College of Physicians advises its tutors at district level that senior house officers should have a formal educational programme taking place in time protected from clinical duties on one half-day each week. The College would expect the new regional offices to regulate trusts, if necessary, in order to ensure that clinical activities were organised in a way that allowed this. Not only must there be protected time for young doctors to learn, but protected time for consultants to teach.

Postgraduate deans may best be affiliated with undergraduate medical schools, and in the new regions which contain more than one medical school, it will be necessary to define their territorial responsibilities.

Continuing medical education

The continuing education of consultants through a professional life in this grade is an essential feature of an effective health service. Again this involves setting aside sufficient time for the acquisition of new knowledge and skills. The Colleges may be able to monitor this, but regulation may be required of trusts that do not acknowledge the necessity of continuing medical education to the long-term success of the NHS.

The NHS and medical schools

Undergraduate education is the responsibility of the universities and the General Medical Council rather than the Colleges, but it is clear that purchasers will need to liaise with medical schools so that medical education can be planned coherently with service delivery. The Colleges are interested in the financial supplements to hospitals that undertake undergraduate teaching and research commonly known as SIFTR. The Colleges would wish to be assured that trusts were financially accountable, and if necessary, regulated to ensure that SIFTR money was directed towards teaching and research and not used to subsidise costs to help trusts win more contracts. However, purchasers also have a role in ensuring that SIFTR is appropriately used; this should not be left to regulation alone.

Research and development

The research and development initiative of the NHS Management Executive has got off to a good start, with 13 out of 14 of the old regional health authorities having appointed directors of research and development, and presumably these functions will be absorbed into the new regional offices. Much clinical research depends upon the recruitment of patients with particular clinical characteristics into randomised controlled trials. It is essential that such initiatives continue in order to advance our knowledge and to expand the treatment options that we can offer our patients. There is, at present, limited financial incentive for purchasers to send patients to tertiary centres for appropriate study. Purchasers need to accept a longer term responsibility to research and development in the health service, and consider how best to develop a secure patient base for clinical studies. Urgent consideration needs to be given as to how best to maintain national initiatives in research and development in a market which is, by its very nature, small-scale and fragmented. How distinct should money for patient care be kept from money for NHS research? How can projects funded by the Medical Research Council, the Association of Medical Research Charities and other bodies best link into hospitals and other care settings funded by a number of different purchasers?

Appointing consultants

Some trust chief executives may take the view that the mix of professional skills to provide an economic service that will win contracts is a matter for them, and for local advice. Advertisements have appeared, in the past few months, for doctors to undertake unsupervised professional work of a type usually considered to be undertaken by a consultant, but without the requirement that applicants have necessarily followed the required course of training. The terms and conditions of service have not been those of the consultant grade and, most important, the appropriate College regional adviser has not been consulted to ensure that the post provides the right opportunities and environment for professional practice of high quality. It has been necessary also to remind such trusts that the appointment of a consultant is governed by a statutory instrument that requires the presence, on advisory appointments committees, of an independent College assessor. A working group chaired by Dr Deirdre Hine, Chief Medical Officer for Wales, has recently explored the functions of advisory appointments committees,[3] but the Colleges believe that the function of the new regional offices must include the regulation of trusts in matters of medical staffing, including the manner of advertisement and appointment, and the terms and conditions of service.

Provision and audit of specialised services

The adequate provision of supra-district services such as neonatal intensive care or neurosurgical services depends upon coherent purchasing for substantial populations. It is clearly in a purchaser's interests to join with others in contracting with relatively few providers with large capital investments, high technical skills and large volumes of work, and thereby better outcomes. However, a purchaser could destabilise a successful specialist provider unit with the aim of improving geographical access for its population by purchasing in preference local care, but ignoring long-term effects. This is an example of where some sort of regulatory action may be required to balance the trades-off of access to and volume in different provider units. Another example of needed regulation might be for the regional offices to take note of regional variations in outcomes,[4] or in service provision,[5] and require sluggish purchasers to take appropriate action to improve services. The clinical audit of supra-district services is another area that must be overseen at regional level, and some sort of regulation may be required in order to ensure that, for example, data for clinical audit were collected in a standardised way.

Conclusion

Health professionals and the Royal Colleges understand the present need to clarify the functions of the various constituent bodies of the new NHS, and trust that this and in particular the clarification of the regulatory functions will proceed with urgency. Their central role in the provision of care requires that they be party to such discussions now, and that a strong medical advisory system is available to, and heeded by the new regional offices.

References

1. Department of Health. *Managing the new NHS.* London: Department of Health, 1993.
2. Department of Health. *Hospital doctor: training for the future.* Report of the Working Group on Specialist Training. London: Department of Health, 1993.
3. Department of Health *Report of the Joint Working Party on the review of appointment of consultants.* London: Department of Health.
4. McColl AJ, Gulliford MC. *Population health outcome indicators for the NHS: (a) A feasibility study. (b) A consultation document.* London: Faculty of Public Health Medicine, 1993.
5. Clinical Standards Advisory Group. *Access to and availability of coronary artery bypass grafting and coronary angioplasty.* London: HMSO, 1993.

9 | A concluding view

Rudolf Klein
Professor of Social Policy, School of Social Science, University of Bath

First, I believe that the notion of 'the market' in the title of this book has to be disaggregated. If we imagine combining on a grid the points made by Clive Smee about the different degrees of competition and by Ian Carruthers about the geographical differences, we end up with not just one market but several different kinds of markets.

The whole question of whether we think competition is desirable has been skirted. We are agreed that it is not an end in itself but a means. We have skirted around the question as to where it is an *appropriate* means. Is competition equally appropriate in all the different markets? There has been talk about collaboration, co-operation and so on, but these are different from competition. I am sure that both concepts are of use somewhere in the National Health Service (NHS) but our understanding needs to be developed of where it is appropriate to encourage competition, and where co-operation rather than competition is desirable.

One simple message coming out from many studies on outcomes and the discussion on quality is that mass production is best. By and large, the more a surgeon does, the safer he or she is. This has some implications for competition: the safest form of treatment would be one national centre dealing with many thousands of cases. If we acknowledge this, we should be careful in engaging in easy rhetoric about competition.*

Another issue is how far we take the longer-term view, and which particular specialties need a long planning horizon to set up a particular facility. There will be enormous variations from service to service. Ease and costs of exit and entry to the market need to be considered, not in a general sort of way, but specialty by specialty and locality by locality, because these will vary.

With regard to regulation, economists tend to argue that the

Editor's note: Health care managers and health policy analysts often use surgical examples to illustrate their points. Physicians are concerned that the concept of the market is less easily translated to supportive management, reassurance and care, all highly valued by patients.

more competition there is, the less the regulation needed. On the whole, the evidence from health care markets is that this proposition does not hold. There is strong evidence from the USA that the more the competition, the more the regulation. We may start to ask *why*. This leads to some interesting conclusions about the kind of regulation that might be considered. We all talk about purchaser–provider split but, to my mind, the split between customers and purchasers is even more interesting and important in the present system. We have a series of agents for the customers, for example, fundholding general practitioners and health authorities. One of the big questions is how effective they are as agents.

There is potential scope for collusive behaviour between purchasers and providers. I would argue that there are strong incentives for purchasers and providers to get together and think of ways of outwitting the NHS Management Executive by cutting corners, possibly by cutting standards, and so on. It is because of this risk of collusive behaviour that we then move to the whole question of the public interest, the common good. One case for managerial oversight of purchasers is to stop them betraying their agency on the patients' behalf. It certainly cannot be taken for granted that they will be effective agents and, as suggested above, there may actually be some incentives for them to betray their trust.

In talking about moving towards regulation of standards—using the word in the proper sense, as opposed to talking most of the time about planning, management and so on—we are talking about evoking the notion of the public interest. The health care market is different because of lack of knowledge and asymmetry of information, in that the customer has to be protected by the basic safety of the product. By that I mean that as a potential customer I want to know that my prospective surgeon does not have a fatality rate of 64%. In the same way, when I buy a television set I want to know that there is not a 64% chance that it will blow up and set my house on fire. Clearly, this is all the more important in health care because it is what health economists call an 'experienced good': that is, an individual suffers the real consequences of, and gets his knowledge of, good or poor service only by being a patient.

Product safety and standards are factors of which we would be in favour in all markets. Where the health care market is different is that we are surely also interested in product mix and range. For example, it is of no public concern if Marks and Spencer discontinues a particular line, the assumption in the market being that the customer will then go somewhere else and find a substitute. However, if a purchaser of health services were to discontinue a particular line—for example, services for severe learning disabilities or some expensive service—there would surely be an element of public interest. The issue of equity, that Alan Maynard raises on p. 18, also comes into any discussion on product range.

It is only at the margins of purchasing that decisions are being taken about the range of services being offered. For example, some authorities have stopped offering *in vitro* fertilisation; in other words, we are moving away from a standard NHS 'menu' of services. Should individual purchasers be free to determine the NHS menu, or is there a public interest in determining what should be offered?

Finally, it is an illusion to think that some sort of formula will be found which will give us a comfortable feeling after some years that we have 'arrived', and that we need no longer worry about turbulence. It was possible to predict in the mid-1980s that there would be big changes in the NHS, simply by looking at other big industrial organisations. After all, the NHS is, among other things, a big industrial organisation and its turbulence is nothing special. We have had turbulence in the universities for the last ten years, and are certainly not yet in a steady state.